SO MANY HATS!

Missionary Stories from the Belgian Congo

Carol and Margie Cross in front of the mud block house at Mangungu

By Margie Wall

Copyright © 2017 by Margie Wall

so many hats!
Missionary Stories from the Belgian Congo
by Margie Wall

Printed in the United States of America.

ISBN 9781498496445

All rights reserved solely by the author. The author guarantees all contents are original and do not infringe upon the legal rights of any other person or work. No part of this book may be reproduced in any form without the permission of the author. The views expressed in this book are not necessarily those of the publisher.

Scripture quotations taken from the New King James Version (NKJV). Copyright © 1997 by Thomas Nelson, Inc. Used by permission. All rights reserved.

www.xulonpress.com

Contents

Foreword xi
Preface xiii
Introduction xv

PART I *In the Kwilu District* 17

  1. Christmas Salt 19
  2. Unnamed Terrors! 23
  3. Kifwanzondo 27
  4. Arriving at Mangungu 31
  5. Daddy Answers Questions 33
  6. Missionary Dentist? 37
  7. The Torpedo 39
  8. The Kite That Flew Without Wind 41
  9. The Saga of the Red Seeds 43
 10. Breaking the Jigger Record 47
 11. Margie Goes to School 49
 12. The Mango Tree 55
 13. Archie the Cook 59
 14. When Bad Things Happen 61
 15. The Cow That Refused to Cross the River . 63
 16. How the Chicken Saved Mulongo 65
 17. Problem Solving – Congo Style 67
 18. Hazards of a Congo Picnic 69
 19. Chief Masud Comes to Church 71

so many hats!

20. Beware the Village Stew 75
21. Twenty Uses for a Palm Tree 77
22. Mom's "Cliff Hangers" 81
23. Last Flight 85
24 Here Comes the Mailman! 89
25 Our New Stone House 95
26 Bearing Fruit 99
    Photo Section 103

PART II *In the Kivu Province* 113

27. A Day in the Life of a Truck 119
28. Christmas in Popokebaba 123
29. New Year's at Mangungu 127
30. When the Jungle Ferry Broke Loose 131
31. Lessons From a Ditch 133
32. "Please Come to Our Village" 135
33. What's in a Move? 139
34. Soldier Ants in the Walls 143
35. The Baboon and the Broomstick 145
36. Mama's 39th Birthday 147
37. *Openglopish* and Other Dialects 149
38. Mama Cross 153
39. Daddy Kitoko Cross 155

Appendix: Languages of Congo 157
About the Author: My Story 159
In Grateful Recognition 161
Related Books on Congo Missions 163

Index of Maps:
    Map of Congo 17
    Map of the Kwilu District 18
    Map of the Kivu Province 113

Contents

Index of Illustrations by Margie Wall:
> *"You pulled the wrong tooth!"* 36
> *Killing the jiggers before church* 46
> *The mango tree* 54
> *Archie builds his first fire in the oven* 58
> *Mom finds rat parts in her stew* 74
> *"Here comes the mailman"* 88
> *Dad's homemade washing machine* 94
> *Women bring their "mambus" to Mom* 98
> *Christmas in the Catholic guest house* 126
> *Soldier ants take over* 142

*In loving memory of my parents,
Ira and Carol Cross,
who modeled God's love
and faithfulness to me.*

Foreword

The book you are holding is an intriguing and eye-opening journey into the world of missions! You will rejoice in the lives of missionaries in the Belgian Congo in the 1940s and 1950s.

Margie, an MK (missionary kid), arrived at Multnomah School of the Bible in 1959 and was soon befriended by a DK (deacon's kid). The DK happened to be my sister, Joyce, who brought Margie home to visit for a weekend in 1960. My parents and siblings welcomed Margie into our family over fifty-five years ago, and she has been a part of our family ever since.

As a 12-year-old, I was fascinated by Margie's stories of Africa and her zest for life. Later, when her parents, Al and Carol Cross, came to our home, I was enthralled by their wholehearted commitment to reaching the world with the gospel. This was revealed in their captivating stories. I feel that part of my view of life and my commitment to God's work was shaped through these relationships.

The uniqueness of this book is that its author is taking you back to her early childhood experiences in the Belgian Congo. She draws on her parents' journals and letters, but the vitality comes from it being her story as well. This is a book you will have trouble putting down. Every story seemed to bring my wife to tears as she considered God's greatness, goodness and grace. You will get a greater appreciation for how God is at work in our world. You should more easily be able to see God at work in your own life.

Rev. Glen N. Eickmeyer
Missions Pastor
First Baptist Church
Eugene, Oregon

Preface

 $\mathscr{I}$ think if any one thing characterized our home life, it was love. I base this statement on the fact that I saw love between my parents, Ira and Carol Cross, and I saw their love toward me as an only child for twenty years, and then I saw their love to my sisters, Cherie and Jeannie, who came later. But most of all, I saw their love for the Lord.

In their late twenties, my parents dedicated themselves to His service. They spent most of the remainder of their lives in Africa doing missionary work, wearing many hats. No missionary in those early days went outdoors without wearing a pith helmet or other hat for protection against sunstroke. That was a given, but the hats I am talking about here are the hats of preachers, mechanics, cooks, doctors, dentists, builders, teachers and hunters.

This book is a collection of stories from my parents' first two terms of service in Congo: four years with Congo Gospel Mission in the Kwilu District followed by three years with Berean Mission in the Kivu Province. My parents returned to Congo in 1960 but never got to the interior because Congo Independence and the violence accompanying it happened first. My parents were evacuated, never to return to Congo. However, they did serve four years in the country of Dahomey (now Benin) with Sudan Interior Mission, doing mostly construction and mechanical work. Their last term of service in

Africa was with the Conservative Baptist Foreign Mission Society, building "Camp Higher Ground," a missionary retreat in the mountains of Ivory Coast. They returned to the States in 1979 and eventually retired in Sonora, California.

My parents both went to their eternal home in 2012 within months of each other. They had celebrated their 72nd anniversary the week before Mom passed away. Dad followed her five months later.

May your own faith be encouraged as you read these accounts of God at work in the Belgian Congo in the early days of missions.

Margie Wall

Introduction

My parents, Ira "Al" and Carol Cross, were both born in 1917 and raised in Christian homes. Dad grew up in Ceres, California. Mom's family moved to Ceres when she was in high school. Although attracted to each other, they didn't date until after graduation. In 1939, having no money for a wedding, they borrowed gas money and eloped to Arizona to get married. Dad went into the Navy in 1943 and served on a weather ship in the Pacific. He was seasick most of the time they were at sea. Once in desperation, he told the Lord, "If you get me out of this, I'll serve You." At the same time back home, my Mom had dedicated her life to the Lord's service.

Dad was eventually discharged from the Navy, and at the age of 29, my parents both attended Denver Bible Institute for one year and then Multnomah School of the Bible in Portland, Oregon, for another year. At the close of that time, they felt the Lord's leading to go to Congo under Congo Gospel Mission, based in Chicago, Illinois. After being accepted in May of 1948, my parents moved to Colorado for more training at Denver Bible Institute. That same year found them planning their departure, and the whole month of July they spent packing. Sundays they spoke at churches, sharing their vision for Congo.

By the end of July, they were fully supported and were ready and eager to go to New York. Their sailing date was August 28, 1948. But they had no funds to get them from California to New York or from New York to Congo. I, too, was ready and eager to go and had my own little suitcase packed.

We were not surprised when a church in Southern California gave an offering that took us as far as Oklahoma where a gift from Dad's Aunt Rose took us on to Denver. A church there gave what we needed to travel to Chicago. At mission headquarters, enough money had come in to get us to New York, but we still had nothing toward the boat passage to Congo. A church in Grand Rapids, Michigan, asked my parents to speak. Dad had spoken there previously, and at that time, the missions committee had offered to "make up whatever was lacking in passage" when the fare had to be paid. Little did they know that "whatever was lacking" would end up being the entire amount! The church kept its word, however, and paid it all.

Our visas arrived the day before we were to sail, another miraculous provision of God. Arriving in Congo at the port city, Matadi, we lacked enough money to travel inland by riverboat to our assigned station. Once more the Lord heard our prayers. There at Matadi, God conveniently had a missionary from the Congo Inland Mission, Mr. Frank Enns, who had to drive right past our station, 500 miles inland. We were able to ride with him in his pickup to Mangungu. When we finally arrived at our destination, my parents had five dollars of cash left.

Yes, for us, this first trip to Congo was one of miracles all the way and a real experience in faith. You will see this thread of faith weave through the following pages. I have attempted a somewhat chronological account depicting our seven years in the Belgian Congo.

Margie Wall

PART ONE

*In the Kwilu District of Belgian Congo
September 1948 to April 1952*

Map of Belgian Congo Provinces

Map of Missions in Kwilu District

1.

Christmas Salt

When my parents first went to the Belgian Congo in 1948, they joined a work Anton and Viola Anderson had established more than 30 years earlier. The Andersons risked much to pioneer in this pagan and primitive country, enduring many privations for the sake of the gospel. The following account by Viola tells about their first Christmas in Congo in 1918. She wrote:

"*It appeared that it would be a flourless, sugarless, and salt less Christmas…. We were getting used to going without flour and sugar, but oh, how hungry we were for salt in our food! We prayed that God would send us some salt by Christmas time….and trusted the Lord to supply this need.*

The afternoon before Christmas a native[1] came to us with a letter and a package from a single missionary man stationed two days' journey north of us. He wrote that someone had sent him a doll head in a package as a joke. Immediately he thought of 'the little white child.' Emma, [our three-year-old

---

[1] *The term "native" has since become derogatory, but at that time it was commonly used to refer to the indigenous peoples.*

daughter] *was the only white child in this part of the Congo at that time, so she was given that name. He thought she ought to have a doll for Christmas, so he set to work to make a body for the doll head. Then he sent it on in haste so that Emma would get it by Christmas.*

When we opened the package, Emma saw the doll and begged for it, so we gave it to her. After she had played with it for a little while, she said, 'Oh, Mamma, my dolly is leaking.' There was a stream of fine, white table salt sifting through the seams. It did not take me long to remove the salt and replace it with rags. Our hearts praised our loving Heavenly Father for answering our prayers for Christmas salt in such a wonderful way.

Later when we told the missionary who had sent the doll of God's answer to prayer, he said, 'When I was planning to fix the doll, I had no trouble in deciding that the best thing to use for the body and dress was unbleached muslin, but to find something with which to stuff the doll was a problem. I walked through all my rooms several times, viewing all of my possessions, for a possible solution to my problem. Then my eyes lit on my box of salt, and I knew immediately that my problem was solved.'"[2]

When we first arrived in Congo, I was seven years old. The "little white girl" in the story above, Emma, now was an adult, married to Angus Brower with four children of her own: Johnny, David, Ruthie and Mary. The Browers were also missionaries with Congo Gospel Mission. David and I attended boarding school together at a Mennonite missionary children's school.

Many times as a child, I saw God answer my parents' prayers. I wonder how many times Emma thought about

---

[2] *Gleam of Light*, by Viola P. Anderson, published 1949 by Congo Gospel Mission, Villa Park, Illinois (page 24).

that Christmas salt-doll and how God had answered her parents' prayers. How true is the verse *"My God shall supply all your need according to His riches in glory by Christ Jesus" (Philippians 4:19).*

2.

Unnamed Terrors!

In 1948, just the words "Belgian Congo" and "Africa" could strike terror in the hearts of the ignorant and faithless. I had two great-aunts who fit that category. When they learned that my parents, Ira and Carol Cross, were going to Africa as missionaries and were taking me (a first grader), they relentlessly tried to dissuade Mom and Dad. They were convinced that the stories (including Tarzan) about "dark Africa" were all true. To them, naked pagans and wild animals were rampant and lurked behind every hut and palm tree.

They often did this in my hearing, and their descriptive pleading filled my head with visions of elephants trampling me, drooling lions tearing me apart and slithering snakes squeezing me to death. I began having nightmares of wild and ferocious animals snarling and growling under my bed and snakes slithering on the floor. *(I still occasionally have these nightmares!)*

But my parents, praise God, stood firm in the call they had received from God to go to the Belgian Congo in Africa and take the gospel to its people. The terrors we ultimately encountered in "dark Africa" were not induced by wild animals but were of an entirely different nature.

Our Ship, the S.S. Vingt, a Belgian ship (formerly a US Liberty ship), docked September 12, 1948, at Matadi, the Congo port city, and disgorged us and our many barrels and cases of freight. The "terrors" that faced us were the red tape necessary to assemble our baggage (it was scattered somehow in several warehouses), pass it through duty, and arrange transportation inland for a 500-mile trip – all while not knowing French, the country's official language. Our senses were disoriented by the heat, humidity and smells of this tropical country. My parents struggled for days to find people who knew English to help them through the morass of baggage claim, customs, lodging and transportation. Finally, the ordeal was nearly over; only one crate was still missing.

Mom and I were standing in one of the warehouses while Dad was negotiating in frustrated sign language when I saw a piece of chalk on the ground near a crate and picked it up. Mom saw it too, and ever the practical woman, figured if there was one, there might be more. Actually, chalk was something we needed, having been unable to find any for my slate. So we seriously searched in all the spaces we could reach between the crates. We did not find any more chalk, but we *did* find the missing crate!

Soon Dad arranged transportation inland with Mr. Enns, a missionary who was traveling inland with a pickup, and we were on our way to the place where my parents were called to serve. The four of us were crowded into the cab of Mr. Enns' pickup. The heat, dysentery, strange culture, insects and narrow dirt roads all contributed to make this a memorable trip.

We never saw an elephant or a lion in Congo, and although we did see snakes, scorpions, gorillas, wild boars and other animals, none were ever a threat to our lives. We came to love the half-naked people of the Bampende tribe with whom we were to live, and my parents saw lives changed as the light of the gospel penetrated the darkness. My parents were faithful to their calling to "*go into all the world and preach the gospel to every creature"* as Christ commanded His disciples in Mark 16:15.

3.

Kifwanzondo

Congo Gospel Mission had five stations in the Kwilu District of the Belgian Congo with headquarters at Tshene. My parents were assigned to Mangungu, the only station unoccupied by missionaries at that time. However, because we needed orientation and also were waiting for our baggage to come by riverboat from Matadi, the mission sent us to Kifwanzondo. There Harry and Vickie Buerer, along with their four daughters (during the furlough of missionaries Angus and Emma Brower), helped introduce us to Congo and its people.

We arrived at Kifwanzondo on Saturday, September 25, 1948. Sunday we attended our first Congo church service along with about 25 nationals. Harry Buerer conducted the service and led the singing. One of the first hymns they sang in *Kikongo* was *"Kwiza kwa Yesu"* (Come to the Savior). It brought tears to Dad's eyes as he recalled wonderful times of singing at Ladd Hill Community Church where he had preached while attending Multnomah School of the Bible. The song had been a favorite there. Mom wrote, "We couldn't understand a word of the message, but we felt the Lord's presence and felt at home." By the next service, Dad had pulled out his C-melody saxophone and participated in the music.

Learning the language, visiting the villages with the Buerers, and participating in worship and prayer meetings helped my parents begin to feel part of this new country. But they wanted so much to get started on their own station. One day they decided to walk the twelve miles to Mangungu just to see it. Mom wrote in her journal: "At 9:30 we started to walk to Mangungu. At every village we walked through, children followed us for a mile or so. We felt like pied pipers! The two porters who went with us to carry our cots and groceries didn't think white people could make it on foot. They were almost right – by the time we stopped at the last rise and could see down to Mangungu, we fully agreed with them. We had blisters (and jiggers) in our feet and were exhausted. We had just started downhill when we heard a car coming. It turned out to be the Andersons from Tshene who had come to tell us that our loads had arrived at the river port. They would take us there to arrange for the transport inland of our things."

While at Tshene waiting for a truck to take the loads, my parents stayed in the station guesthouse. Here, Mom got another introduction to Congo. With no closet in the room, Mom hung her dress over the rafters that night. The next morning, she found it covered with big black ants that had eaten small holes in it.

Also at Tshene, Dad began his ministry of fixing things, a career for which he was to become famous during the four years he lived in this part of Congo. Not one to sit idle, he made an accordion case from an old suitcase for one of the missionary ladies (the original case had burned in a house fire), worked on a motorcycle and repaired a phonograph.

We went to the port when word came that a truck had been located to deliver our things. Mom described the unloading process from the barge: "There are two boards from the barge to the bank (one for porters going up, and one for the ones coming down). Our baggage had been put in a bamboo pole warehouse. In loading our boxes and barrels from the warehouse to the truck, one man carried 280 pounds – on his back. Another one tried for our woodstove (340 pounds), but his knees sagged!" The 115-mile jolting trip to Mangungu with more than two tons of luggage was uneventful (a rare thing in Congo). *Now we Crosses were ready to arrive at Mangungu. Or were we?*

4.

Arriving at Mangungu

November 5, 1948, the hired truck took us to Mangungu. When Archie Haller, the first missionary there, passed away, his wife, Ella, and daughter, Genevieve, moved to Intshuem to begin an orphanage, leaving Mangungu vacant for several years.

Mom wrote about our arrival: "We arrived at Mangungu at 3:30 p.m. and had *"mingi-mingi"* (many, many) native helpers to unload the truck. What furniture we had they quickly carried into the house. The house is the one the orphans lived in before they moved to Intshuem. It has three main rooms; the middle one is a screened living room. A makeshift bathroom lies off the bedroom. While we were digging out linens and things to cook with, we found a large native making the beds with hospital corners and all! He was tall with a raffia skirt and hair in mud rolls. (It turns out that he once had been a houseboy for a missionary.)

"The next day (Saturday), we opened all the remaining crates with lots of help and with every square inch of window screen occupied by onlookers. Everything we unpacked was accompanied with many "oh's" and "ahs." We had to put our wood cook stove together, patch some pipe for it and attach it to the chimney. This was in a small one-room building several yards from the back door of the house.

"Sunday morning we ate hot cocoa and leftover sandwiches from the trip. Got ready for the 9 a.m. church service in an open building (grass roof and dirt floor with bamboo benches). A Christian native teacher had been maintaining services since the missionaries left. We got there early, and Ira warmed up his saxophone while the crowd filtered in. We sat on the front bench, which promptly broke! [This happened periodically in the years to come.] We sang some well-known hymns in *Kikongo*. The teacher opened the service in prayer. Then he gave a message from Luke 5:17 about the lowering of the sick man through the roof to Jesus. Because we knew the story, we were able to follow along with his intonations and gestures. There were probably 120 people present, all curious about us. Everyone wanted to shake our hands. We learned quickly how to do it their way: You shake hands, then grasp thumbs and then shake hands again!

"Monday we set about hiring some water boys to carry drinking and wash water from a spring. We hired two other men to cut and bring firewood for our stove. We also installed the kerosene refrigerator and got it working.

"You might ask, 'What is the Mangungu station like?' It is located on a square, ten-acre plot just off the Idiofa-Yassa road, halfway between the villages of Mangungu and Luembe, about a mile apart. The station grounds are well laid out although greatly overgrown. Palms line the main paths. We have two coconut palms, some date palms and fifty oil palms. There are six mango trees, eight guava trees, several star fruit trees, forty-three citrus trees (grapefruit, limes, lemons and tangerines), sixteen avocado trees, some coffee trees and two-hundred pineapple plants.

"There is so much to do! We must learn the *Kikongo* language. We must maintain the school and the station compound. We must learn the culture of these tribes so we can minister to them. We need to get a flushing toilet and a vehicle and more kerosene (our fridge has run out). But in spite of all this, or maybe because of it, *we would not exchange our place here for anywhere in the world!*"

5.

Daddy Answers Questions

From a letter to his Aunt Rose in America on December 28, 1948, four months after leaving the United States and about six weeks after arriving at Mangungu.

"Dear Aunt Rose – To answer your questions, our house has a grass roof. The walls are made of hand-made sun-dried clay bricks, which wash away in the rain, so we have a four-foot wide verandah that wraps the house. This also makes the house cooler because the direct sun cannot strike inside. The walls are plastered with gray river clay. We hope to re-plaster them with cement when we get enough money to do it. Our house now has a rough cement floor that we would like to cover with a smooth coat. The ceilings are split bamboo mats.

"To speak frankly of the sanitary situation, it is not very good. We do have an inside toilet, which is a hand-molded cement stool with a cement six-inch tube going down and just outside the wall where it dumps into the seep hole. Nearly all white men's houses here have these hand-made stools. They beat the outside privies immensely, but the drawback is that making a satisfactory water trap is impossible; so the fumes are sometimes terrific and *always* bad. The flies go in, and the bugs come out, and periodically the white worms make a pilgrimage into the daylight!

"I heard from a missionary going through the other day that they now have some American-made toilets in Kikwit (about 90 miles away). With a 55-gallon drum just outside the wall to pipe in water for flushing, the system would work for us. We will definitely be getting one of these as soon as we can. We have no car yet; so getting the toilet may take awhile. Our hand-molded cement washbasin is very usable as is our cut-in-half-lengthwise steel drum bathtub. We carry buckets of hot water (heated on our wood stove) for baths.

"About furniture. Our mission director had his carpenters make me eight square table legs and side pieces, and I used the 1x12 boards from our crates to make two very serviceable tables. The director also gave us a handmade double bed with woven cane springs. It sags in the middle but is comfortable enough with the quilted mattress a church in Littleton, Colorado, gave us to bring here. We bought three camp cots to use on our trip across Congo, and Margie now sleeps on one of them. The other two we use for guests.

"The clothes closet in our bedroom is the refrigerator carton our kerosene fridge came in. One side is cut out, and a bamboo pole running through it serves as a clothes rod. Everything wooden in our house has to be set up on tin cans and at least two inches from the wall to foil white termite ants. We cook with a wood stove that is fueled by wood carried by a native workman. The kerosene we ordered has not yet arrived, but another missionary gave us five gallons so we can use our lamps at night.

"It is rainy season, and so the air is very humid. The quinine we take as a malaria prophylactic is not too bad when you regulate the daily dose so it is enough to keep the malaria in check but not enough to make the ears ring too badly. We usually take five grains a day, which we load into the capsules ourselves. If we feel a fever coming on, then we take another five as a 'cure.'

"We use stream water from about three-fourths of a mile away. Two men carry the water, two buckets each on a pole across their shoulders. A palm frond lying on top of the water keeps it from sloshing out when they climb the hill with full buckets. They make three trips for one franc (about two cents). We must boil the water well before we drink it, or it will give us diarrhea. We are beginning to realize that a car is a necessity here, but it is up to the Lord to move in His good time.

"We are on the border of two tribal tongues – the Bampendes in the first village to the north and the Bambundas to the south. If you wish to talk with the women, you must learn these tribal tongues. *Kikongo* is the trade language and spoken by the men only. Because it is a commercial built-up language for trade purposes, it is starved for expressive vocabulary. Margie is learning the languages quickly because she is unafraid to talk to the natives. Our Christian cook, Archie, has a baby about three months old, that Margie carries everywhere.

"Christmas has come and gone for another year. Last Sunday morning was Christmas, and with it came one of those high points that come scarcely in a lifetime. It was the first time for me in the pulpit using another language, a privilege and experience not given to all servants of the Lord. Homiletically speaking and in limited vocabulary, it was a flop, but the Word was given out, and the way of salvation proclaimed. We know that God will accomplish His purposes through it. We thank the Lord over and over for you and those who have made it possible for us to be here. You shall have your part in the reward!

"The day before Christmas, we gave clothes to over seventy boys and girls in school who have never had anything but a loin cloth before. This is the generation coming up under the sound of the gospel from day to day that will become the solid Christians of tomorrow when they accept Christ, for they are getting groundwork in the Scriptures now.

       Love, Ira and Carol and Margie"

"You pulled the wrong tooth!"

6.

Missionary Dentist?

    In 1949, the Belgian Congo in Africa had few practicing dentists. The tribe my parents worked with in the Kwilu District of lower Congo was still quite primitive. The women dressed topless and wore hand-woven raffia skirts that they never washed. They were required to wear tops when attending church, which they did, but they were so uncomfortable that they removed them as soon as they left the building! They loved jewelry and usually wore many metal or bead bracelets, necklaces and earrings. Their hairdos often formed a pointed topknot from which they rolled all the hair in mud and oil (I think) to make stiff, dangling ringlets. I don't know the exact mud formula, but it was smelly!

    Another beauty feature of this particular tribe was filing the front teeth to points. This often led to decay and infection, and already in the first year they were at Mangungu, Dad realized that to work with these people he would have to learn how to pull teeth. However, not having proper dental forceps, the first teeth he pulled were with sterilized automotive pliers! Hearing of this, his Aunt Rose sent him some dental tools. Mind you, Dad was able to do many things, but with no medical training, dentistry was a new hat for him. He eventually set up a dispensary with designated hours for treating ulcerated feet (from jiggers), wounds, malaria, worms and other ailments. In those days, missionaries did whatever was needed to minister to the people physically as well as spiritually.

When pulling teeth with no anesthetic available, Mom and Dad – in their ignorance – gave the patient an aspirin and proceeded immediately with the extraction without allowing the aspirin time to take effect. The Congolese people, however, were stoic about pain and seldom complained.

I distinctly remember one elderly woman who came with an ailing tooth. She brought a basket of eggs in payment for the extraction[3]. By now, Dad had forceps, making his job easier. He pulled the tooth she indicated. After she had spit a good amount of blood on the ground, she broke into a full grin and turned to Dad and informed him that he *had pulled the wrong tooth!* Undaunted, she pointed to another tooth, which Dad also extracted. She was, ironically, as happy as she could be and went away cackling gleefully. After all, she had gotten two teeth pulled for the price of one!

This story is part of the reason that I am calling this collection of missionary stories "So Many Hats." Missionaries in the early days in primitive areas were called to wear many hats, doing things way out of their comfort zones because there was no one else to do them. My parents taught the Bible, taught elementary and secondary school classes, treated ulcers and other ailments, delivered babies, gave CPR, pulled teeth, repaired phonographs and bicycles, led music, built buildings, hauled water, buried people, repaired their own cars, taught agriculture, hunted and canned wild meat, and baked their own bread, just to name a few of the "hats."

How did they do it? They did it in God's strength, because *when God calls, He enables and equips.*

---

[3] *Eggs were often used as barter or even placed in the offering plate.*

7.

The "Torpedo"

The "Torpedo," as Dad nicknamed it, was a well-used 1928 Model A Ford and our first car in the Belgian Congo. Dad bought it in February of 1949 for $400 from Mrs. Near of Vanga who, after seventeen years in Congo without taking a furlough, was finally returning to the States on a doctor's orders. The car was originally a tourist car that Mrs. Near rebuilt into a station wagon to use in her extensive village ministry. She had apparently done most of the repair work herself, including major engine repair. Our need for a vehicle was desperate, having been at the station of Mangungu for five months with no transportation.

Once during the period without a car, we visited Mrs. Haller at her orphanage. Mom and Dad walked, but I was allowed to ride in a *kipoy* (a chair seat suspended between poles that national porters carried). The jostling ride took about two hours.

Not long after he got the Torpedo, Dad realized that to use the car for hauling water barrels and supplies, he needed to convert it to a pickup, which he did by tearing off the roof. But he soon realized we were too exposed, so he added a canvas top over the seat to protect us from the harsh African sun and occasional rain.

Once, Mom asked Dad to park the stripped-down Torpedo in the middle of the station lawn as a model for the school kids to draw in art class. She was not an artist and had no idea how to teach perspective; so she wasn't too surprised when the kids turned in their pictures – most of them with all four wheels in a row on one side of the car! Mom later told me she wished she had asked me to teach that class.

I don't remember the ultimate fate of the Torpedo, but in March of 1950, we upgraded to a more practical and newer vehicle, again purchasing it from missionaries leaving Congo. The car was a 1947 Ford "woody" station wagon, well cared for and a wonderful improvement.

Dad may have parted out the Torpedo at that point. In fact, the gauges I later nailed in my tree house for my cockpit dash may have come from it. David Brower from Kifwanzondo, on one of the occasions his family visited, and I used all kinds of car parts (possibly from the Torpedo) and wood scraps to build a "car" near Dad's shop. Everything on our car was stationary, including the steering wheel and other wheels, but that didn't stop us from "traveling" far and wide! The car had a wooden box for a pickup bed in which we put "freight."

For me, the Torpedo was just a car, but for my parents, it was a means to get supplies from Kikwit or Idiofa, to help other missionaries, or to make emergency trips with the villagers to the doctor. The car was a necessary tool to help them in their missionary work. *Go Torpedo!*

8.

The Kite That Flew Without Wind

We were not surprised when a crowd of village people, including the chief, came panting up the driveway behind our 1928 Model A Ford. This was normal procedure when we returned to the station in the car. Some of the young men had learned that touching the spark plugs while the engine was still running gave them a thrilling shock. They would line up to touch the spark plugs before Dad shut the engine off. He would lift the hinged side of the hood and wait patiently until everyone had his chance. But I'm getting ahead of the story here.

At this time, I was a second grader being taught by Mom. There was a story about a kite in my reader. I had no idea what a kite was; so Mom and Dad took time off and made one – a traditional kite – of sticks, paper and a rag tail. Because there was no wind, Dad decided to drive onto the prairie and let me fly the kite behind the car. I sat in the back and held the string, letting it out behind the moving vehicle. It worked! I gazed up in awe at the kite flying behind us twenty or thirty feet in the air, gracefully soaring and dipping along. Here we were, deep in the bush of the Belgian Congo, and I was having a little taste of normal American childhood. Finally, I pulled the kite in, and we headed home.

Now I can take you back to the arrival at the mission station, where the village people circled the car. But this time they weren't there to touch the spark plugs. Dad was finally able to determine what they were chattering so excitedly about. They wanted to warn us that an evil spirit had been following us all the time we were out! So Dad took the kite from the back of the car and showed them that we had made it. The kite was not an evil spirit but a toy he had made for me to fly.

They understood toys because their children had all kinds of toys. They made cars and trucks out of bamboo that had working wheels and were pulled by a string or pushed with a stick. The children engineered some of the toy cars so that as the wheel went around, it made a ticking noise. They also created toys from sardine and other tin cans. They had hoops they would roll and had games that were played with beans and rocks.

Yes, the villagers understood toys and were relieved that the evil spirit really was just a toy for the white child. But understanding the Good News of Jesus Christ was more difficult. Dad and Mom worked hard to learn the *Kikongo* language and the tribal culture so they could communicate God's love to the Mangungu people.

9.

The Saga of the Red Seeds

In my mother's journals of the early Belgian Congo days, Mom commented several times about how hard it was to get me to do schoolwork. That was because all I wanted to do was play outside, collecting bugs or seeds.

There was a plethora of delightful bugs to collect in tropical Africa. Wasps were not so delightful, but I'd catch them so I could cut their stingers off. The African children and I would catch flying ants to eat. We would pick them off the screen windows by the wings and pop the delicious bacon-flavored bodies into our mouths.

There was also a funny worm-like creature about a half-inch long with a big pincher-type head that dug little "well" holes in wet sand. The driveway in front of our house was sandy and was a great location for these worms. Their eighth-inch diameter holes were easy to spot after a rain, and the African kids taught me how to "go fishing." We'd pull the skin off a palm frond, roll it into string between our palms, spit on one end and then dip it in some drier sand, forming a little ball on the end. This we would drop down the hole until the worm grabbed it. Then we'd quickly yank him out. We would race to see who could catch the most "fish."

Then there were other bugs that came out after a rain (from where I have no idea). I'd get a pie tin from Mom in which to collect them. The bugs were bright red and about a quarter inch in diameter – fuzz balls, a lot like pom-poms. These I would "catch-and-release", returning them to the wild after my pie tin was full.

One of the things I liked most to collect were little seeds that came in pods on a vetch-like plant that grew wild along our driveway. The hard-shelled seeds were bright shiny red with a black dot on one end. They looked a lot like ladybugs. I had jars full of them in my room.

We returned to the States in 1952, and for more than fifty years I never thought about the red seeds again until one day several years ago. My husband and I were returning from a trip to San Francisco, and we stopped to browse at a thrift store in the Eureka area. There on a shelf was a jar with assorted rocks and seed pods in it – including some of those little red seeds! I stood there, transfixed, staring at them. Suddenly I was seven years old and collecting those seeds in Congo. I was squatting beside our sandy driveway wearing my pith helmet. I was sweaty, and my sandaled feet were dirty. The skirt of my dress held a bunch of the seeds. Of course, I bought the jar in Eureka and quickly sorted out the red seeds (about ten). They ended up in a little vial in my jewelry box – just a treasured memory.

In the process of writing this chapter, I became curious. *What were those seeds?* We took one of them in a little zipped plastic bag to the Oregon State Extension Service. Within two days, we had their reply. The seeds are called "rosary peas" (used in rosaries and jewelry in South America). They are actually *deadly*. The poison contained in the seed is *abrin*, a close relative of *ricin*, and one of the most fatal toxins on earth! Jewelry makers have died after pricking a finger while handling a rosary pea.

Killing jiggers before church

The Bampende peoples in our area of Congo believed that when a person died in the village, *someone was responsible for that death*. The witch doctor, with sole authority, would determine who it was. That person would be given a poisoned drink. Could the poison have been derived from the little red seed?

One instance of a mysterious death might have been related. Our laundry boy, Gideon, a Christian lad who testified faithfully in the village of his salvation, died while we were on a trip. Mom wrote that the Christians thought he had been poisoned.

No one ever told us the seeds were poisonous. How many even knew? Why hadn't I done what most children would have done and *tasted* the seeds?

God protected me from crushing or ingesting one of these little seeds!

10.

Breaking the Jigger Record

    December 11, 1949 was a memorable day. I was eight years old. Mom, Dad, and I were living in our mud block house at Mangungu. It was bedtime and we were doing the nightly ritual on Mom and Dad's bed – something we did every night before family devotions. It was called jigger control.

    Jiggers are little six-legged mites common in sub-Sahara Africa. They burrow into the skin of men and animals, suck blood, and cause severe itching. They cause more and worse things if not removed the same day. "More" is the zillion little ones that eventually hatch from the egg sacs the jiggers create around themselves. "Worse" are the infections and diseases that can develop if these mites are not attended to.

    Jiggers live in dry sand and dirt and are carried by pigs and other animals. They happily jump onto human feet at every opportunity. Even though I never went barefoot, the jiggers still got on me. Water discouraged them, and every Sunday morning before church, the school kids sprinkled down the dirt floor of the church with watering cans. That way the jiggers left us alone during church. After watering the dirt floor, the kids beat the hollowed-out log drum in the back of the church to call the villagers.

Every night I crawled onto Mom and Dad's bed for foot inspection. I usually knew where the jiggers were by the redness and itching, but I couldn't remove them by myself. Dad sterilized a needle with a match and dug the jiggers out, daubing the spot with Mercurochrome afterward. Usually I had only a few jiggers and occasionally none, but if I'd been playing outside all day in the dry season, there might have been lots. I can't remember the exact figure, but a number in the twenties comes to mind as the record for jiggers in my feet in a day.

On that December 11 day, after the jigger-digging session, we had family devotions. Dad was reading from John 10 and came to verse 9 (Jesus' words): *"I am the door. If anyone enters by Me, he will be saved…."* I couldn't understand how Jesus was a *door* and said so. Dad had me climb off the bed and walk through the bedroom door into the living room. He then explained how going through that doorway was the only way to get from the bedroom to the living room – just as Jesus was the only way to get from death to life. He went on to tell me the way of salvation in words I could understand. Wow – forget about jiggers! I knew I wanted to walk through that Door to eternal life. And that's the day I prayed to accept Jesus as my Savior.

Jesus also says in Revelation 3:20: *"Behold, I stand at the door and knock. If anyone hears My voice and opens the door, I will come in to him and dine with him, and he with Me."* Is Jesus knocking at your heart's door today?

11.

Margie Goes to School

From a letter by Ira Cross on February 2, 1950

"We trust this finds all of you well and happy in the Lord. We have much to be thankful for. Although after returning from taking Margie to a Mennonite school for missionary children, we find it very quiet here!

"It was, however, far from a quiet trip. We started Thursday afternoon and went to Kifwanzondo to pick up Angus Brower's son David (7), who was, like Margie (8), going away for the first time to boarding school. We left before light the next morning, intending to arrive at Kipungu that evening. The directions we had were to go to Kikwit and then follow the signs to Leopoldville, staying on that road for about 100 miles until we saw the sign to Kipungu.

"At 9 a.m. when we were about two-thirds of the way to Kikwit, a large bug flew around the side of the windshield of our 1928 Model A [the Torpedo] and hit me in the left eye. The impact felt like a one-inch diameter rock coming with the speed of a baseball! I shut both eyes and slammed on the brakes. Carol guided the car to a stop. A half hour passed before I could hold my right eye open enough to drive. When we got to Kikwit, we found a doctor who put some medication in the badly bruised eye and bandaged it. We needed to shop for supplies in Kikwit, which took way longer than planned. By the time we had finished, it was 5 p.m. A missionary we met in Kikwit told us two roads led to Leopoldville — the Bumba ferry road was the shorter, but the Leverville ferry road was the easiest to find. We chose the Leverville ferry road and arrived at the ferry just at dark, barely able to persuade the men to ferry us across.

"Realizing this was yet going to be a long trip, we made beds down in the back for the kids and then pushed on into the night. Going through village after village, we paused only to inquire if we were on the Leopoldville road. When we estimated we had driven eighty or ninety miles, we began asking about Kipungu, but nobody had heard of it. At 10 p.m. we decided to look for a "gite" [a government open house for travelers to camp in]. Some natives told us there was one about two hours' walk ahead of us. While buzzing along toward it, a short circuit developed somewhere in the car's wiring, and the headlights went out. We pushed on with flashlights (held by Carol) and my one good eye. But the mountainous roads were too much, and we finally stopped beside the road, moved David up to the floorboards, put Margie onto the seat, and Carol and I bedded down in the back. Of course we had to unload all our baggage to do that!

"As dawn broke we awoke, combed our hair, brushed our teeth, gassed and oiled the Torpedo and headed down the road. We had not been able to refill our tank and jerry cans in Kikwit because the town was temporarily out of gas. Now, thoroughly lost, without enough fuel to return to Kikwit but trusting the Lord to give us some kind of direction, we drove on. At the next village, the natives told us we were in Baptist territory near Vanga, one of the largest Baptist stations in that part of Congo.

"We had met missionaries from Vanga but did not know where the station was. With uncertain native directions, we arrived about 10 a.m. There Rev. and Mrs. Giddings fed us bacon and eggs, heard our story, and showed us our position on a map. We had come more than a hundred miles northwest when we should have taken the Bumba road and gone about sixty miles southwest! This left us still 120 miles from Kipungu. Why the Lord had let us go this way to arrive at a mission station miles from where we wanted to be, we did not know. But wait....

"As we were saying our goodbyes, Rev. Giddings took one good look at the Torpedo and said, 'You could really use the car we are about to sell because we are going on furlough in a few months.' The car in question was a 1947 Ford station wagon, well taken care of and with new tires. The going price for this model and year would be about 100,000 francs ($2,000). He said I could have it for half of that, but I needed to let him know in a couple months. Now I knew why the Lord had allowed this detour. [We eventually got this car that served us well the rest of that term in Congo.]

"Taking our leave, with a map firmly in hand and many thanks, we drove to the nearest oil post where we obtained full tanks of gas. We arrived at Kipungu just before dark Saturday evening. There are two fine [missionary] couples and two single ladies on this station. Scholastically and spiritually they are well equipped to take care of the training of Margie and the other children. The station's location is ideal; it is five acres on a plateau. The land drops all the way around to the forested village nearly one thousand feet below. But more blessed to us than the view was the Christian fellowship. We stayed over Sunday, disliking traveling on the Lord's Day unless necessary. Leaving there Monday morning, we arrived home again about 6:30 p.m., going the short route of 160 miles!

"Again I say, it is quiet here without Margie, but we know she is in the Lord's hands. Please continue to pray for us here that we may become real missionaries, doing His work in this place.

"Yours in His precious name, Ira and Carol Cross."

The Mango Tree

12.

The Mango Tree

It was a big, magnificent tree that grew in our yard, halfway between the back of our mud-block, thatch-roofed house and the cookhouse. I was an only child, about eight years old, when I made friends with the mango tree. It was a wonderful climbing tree, and in one of the lower horizontal branches, I nailed some old gauges Dad had given me and even attached a steering wheel. This was my "airplane" in which I spent many happy hours "flying" to wonderful imaginary places. A year or two later, Dad built a tree house platform for me about halfway up the tree. From my lofty perch, I had a great view of many of the things that went on around the mission station.

Thinking about that tree and the hours I spent in it got me reflecting on the tree itself and all the things it might have witnessed in its lifetime. It would have seen the time the African teacher came to initiate my parents during their first week in the mud house. He came in full pagan costume, dressed like a *mingantsi*[4] (witchdoctor), whooping and brandishing

---

[4] *Mingantsi* is the title of a type of witch doctor. When a mingantsi was in costume, he would not speak or stop moving. No one was to know his identity.

a machete. When Dad charged out of the house with his rifle, the teacher quickly took off his mask. Once Dad recognized him, they were able to laugh together about it.

At another time while Dad was away, the tree would have seen Mom herself charge out of the house with the rifle to "scare off" the chief's dog that was chasing our chickens. What she thought was a wild shot surprised her by hitting the target! There was quite a palaver before Mom and Dad were able to settle with the chief.

Perhaps one of the most endearing stories the tree could tell was about the ice cube hidden in one of its lower joints. Mom was in the process of defrosting our kerosene refrigerator in the cookhouse. The African workmen were cutting the grass nearby, and she thought they might be refreshed by an ice cube (something new to them). She brought out a tray and handed out the ice cubes. I remember seeing the men tossing them back and forth between their hands and hollering, *"Tiya, tiya!"* (hot, hot). She told them they could eat them.

Some did, but one man carefully wrapped his in a leaf and put it on a low limb of the mango tree. He said he wanted to save it to take home to his wife when he got off work. Mom told him that it wouldn't be there. "Oh, yes it will," he replied. "I will watch it carefully." He could not be convinced that it would disappear until he went to get it a couple hours later and found only water. Mom, the other men, the tree and I all witnessed his surprised exclamation.

I loved that old mango tree. It was actually one of several trees that had been deliberately planted in different seasons so one tree would always be bearing fruit. The trees cycled the seasons, just as God created them. But because Congo is near the equator, we did not have the four seasons; we had summer year round. The trees bore fruit on a cycle that started when each was planted.

We all know that my mango tree couldn't actually *see* the things that happened under and around it. It was unaffected by the Bible studies held in its shade or by the rifle shots fired around its trunk or by the leopards that prowled under it or by the little girl who climbed in its branches. The tree just went on year after year, doing what the Creator had designed it to do. *Ephesians 2:10 says: "For we are God's workmanship, created in Christ Jesus to do good works, which God prepared in advance for us to do" (NIV).*

The mango tree did exactly what God created it to do. We, however, have been given the ability to choose whether or not we will do what God commands. Life would be a lot simpler if we automatically, like the mango tree, did God's will. The prophet Jonah in the Bible is a perfect example of this truth. Had he done God's will and gone to Nineveh directly, he would have avoided spending three days in the stomach of the great fish!

Archie built his first fire in the oven!

13.

Archie the Cook

*A*rchie, a local believer, asked for work as a cook shortly after we arrived at Mangungu. His full name was "Mbaland Archie Robbins." He may have been named after Archie Haller, the founder of the Mangungu mission station. Mom fired him a number of times during the four years we were there but somehow always ended up hiring him back. He was a likeable guy and tried hard to please.

His career as our cook got off to a bad start when he built the first fire in the cook stove *in the oven!* In November of 1948, Mom wrote in her journal: "We have egg trouble. Yesterday, I ordered scrambled eggs. Archie forgot and fried them and then tried to fix it by chopping them with the nut chopper. Today, I ordered them fried; so he beat them. I put those up to make ice cream with. Then he boiled some! I gave up."

From a letter dated December 6, 1948, Mom wrote: "I made cinnamon rolls, but for some reason they wouldn't cook on the bottom. We went to look at the stove and found it full of tar. The stove is fairly new, and the wood we've been burning seemed to be okay. Then we discovered that Archie had been roasting palm nuts in the oven. They make a real tar when roasted. We spent about three hours cleaning the oven. I bawled him out but am too soft-hearted to let him go."

She must have fired him, though, because in a letter a month later she wrote: "Archie is really trying hard since I fired him and then got soft and rehired him. He even made a good white cake today since our order for sugar came."

Later in January of 1950, Mom wrote: "Archie drank some DDT spray from a discarded can he grabbed for a drinking cup. He really gave us a scare. Ira mixed up some mustard and water and made him drink a lot until he vomited and then repeated the process. The next noon, Archie had a high fever, and we were worried. But it turned out to be malaria."

Mom's parents had sent some canned foods in a package. Canned corn was a treat, and Mom asked Archie to heat it to go with supper that day. He thought it was soup, so he added a can of water and served it as soup! Then another time Mom fired Archie for stealing fruit out of our kitchen and supplies from the storehouse, and lying about it. He later confessed and said "God has been giving me pain about it." He was back in the kitchen a month later and in trouble again. He got careless about boiling the drinking water, and Dad got dysentery. Mom took over the drinking water preparation after that.

In another journal entry, Mom wrote: "For breakfast this morning, we *drank cake*! Archie said it was cocoa. We discovered that he had made it from a 'cocoa cake' recipe."

Mom made no further references to Archie. We did find out he had sleeping sickness[5] after a Belgian Sanitary Agent had visited Mangungu to give small pox shots and test the people for sleeping sickness. Perhaps that contributed to Archie's incompetence! But he loved God, and I'm sure he's in Heaven doing perfect cooking!

---

[5] Sleeping sickness ("African trypanosomiasis") is carried by the tsetse fly, common in sub-Sahara Africa. It is a fatal disease unless treated but is curable if diagnosed early enough. It leads to extreme lethargy and eventual death.

14.

When Bad Things Happen....

...Brick machine breaks
...Schoolteachers quit
...Missionary girl dies
...Pilot crashes plane

*T*hese things all happened while I was home from school on summer vacation in July of 1950. For Dad to repair the brick machine, we had to go to the Baptist Mid-Missions station Kandale where there was a welder. So we made plans for the 150-mile trip. Meanwhile, though, tragedy had struck at Kandale. Missionaries Arnold and Pearl Peterson had three boys and a twelve-year-old daughter, Jeannine, who had fallen critically ill with cerebral malaria. Howard Street, a missionary pilot, was flying a doctor and medicine from Kikwit and was still 100 miles from Kandale when he crashed the plane.

The plane, a Piper Cruiser, had been a gift to the mission from R.G. LeTourneau. The plane had landed on a dirt road in the mountains so the pilot could verify directions. Darkness was only about an hour away, after which they would be unable to fly. Normally, landmark navigation is no problem in Congo where many waterways flow through the country, but that day a heavy overcast from prairie fires made visibility less than a mile. On takeoff from the dirt road, the plane fell from about 100 feet altitude. At about the same time the plane went down, Jeannine passed away.

When the plane crashed, the doctor was in the rear seat and sustained only minor injuries. Mr. Street, in the front seat, hit his head on the cowling of the dash. He suffered severe shock and a broken nose. Because of possible internal head injuries, and to prevent blood clots, the doctor ordered extreme quiet for him.

Our arrival at Kandale was timely and served a good purpose while Howard Street was laid up. Dad dismantled the plane and put the parts and motor on a boat at Kikwit bound for Leopoldville. The motor was undamaged, and some of the rest of the plane was recoverable. My parents also gave the Petersons some emotional support in their time of grief. The Petersons had decided to go home to the U.S. for furlough at this time, and we were able to help them practically as well, by taking them to Leopoldville to catch their flight.

We may never know, on this earth, why bad things happen. Did our brick machine break so we would be at Kandale at a time to help the Petersons? Maybe. Sometimes God gives us a glimpse of His plan, but in the case of Jeannine's death, we have no answers. Why would God allow the plane carrying a doctor and the medicine she needed to crash and at the same time take Jeannine?

God is sovereign. He is all-powerful. He is everywhere. He is all-knowing. He could have changed anything about this story, but He chose to let it happen.

Yes, bad things happen, but God brings victory through His power, plan and purpose to ultimately bring glory and honor to Himself. In the case of the Petersons in Congo, we must believe that *"all things work together for good to those who love God, to those who are the called according to His purpose"* (Romans 8:28).

15.

The Cow That Refused to Cross the River

We were still at Kandale. After we helped the Petersons pack up and leave on furlough following the death of their daughter, Jeannine, they gave us a cow. Dad's idea was to hire a cow-sentry to herd it the 150 miles to Mangungu. Dad planned to butcher it there, and Mom would can it. *"A man's heart plans his way, but the Lord directs his steps" (Proverbs 16:9).* This is how the Lord directed our steps that day.

In Dad's own words, from a letter to family in the States: "In the process of trying to get this half-Brahma steer on the ferry to cross the river, it rebelled, and with a terrific lunge smashed me against a big tree trunk. We had tied two ropes around his neck, one to each side with another missionary holding one rope and with me holding the other. My rope was about twenty feet from the steer's head, and a native was holding the loose end behind me. When the man nudged the steer to direct him up the ferry ramp, the steer jumped, reared on his hind legs, made a full turn and came down facing me on his opposite side. My native, following prior orders (unfortunately), pulled hard on his loose end, which bound me to the steer's side. With about five stiff-legged jumps, the steer hit the tree with me in between. I fell to the ground and could only get a little breath at a time. The others had their rope around the tree, pulling the steer until it was snubbed against the tree, and there he stayed until the rope finally broke. Then he walked away.

"Never has the Lord seemed as close as He did for the hour I lay there trying to get my breath. After an interminable time, the other missionary returned from the station with Carol and Margie. Two hours and two morphine injections later, we arrived at the Mukedi Mennonite station for examination by a good missionary doctor. God was good! I had only a few broken ribs. In two weeks we were home at Mangungu."

A few weeks later, Mom wrote: "After taking Margie to school again in September, we went back to Kandale to get the cow – dead this time! We canned ninety pints of beef after filling the top freezer part of our refrigerator. The canned beef is a real treat and a wonderful change from corned beef."

The local people got their protein from many sources that were unappetizing to us – little wild birds, snakes, grubs, grasshoppers, or any wild animal they could kill. Whenever possible, Dad shot game for them and us. We raised chickens, which supplied us with eggs and meat, but oh, what a treat to have beef!

In her letter, Mom continued about the cow: "One lesson we learned: Don't get between a steer and a tree!"

I, Margie, think we learned a lot more than that. As a child, I learned my Daddy was not invincible, but God had protected him from serious injury or even death. I think Mom learned a new level of thankfulness to God for sparing her husband. I also learned that what sometimes seems like an impossible situation always works out – God sends the right people at the right time to help. He never promised to spare us from difficulties, but He does promise to be with us through them. I think all three of us Crosses learned that in 1950. I'd like to think that we all three grew deeper in our walk of faith because of what happened.

16.

How the Chicken Saved Mulongo

A ruckus erupted in the middle of the night from the chicken coop. You who have raised chickens know how loud a ruckus in the chicken coop can be! Dad, his hair on end, barefoot, and in his pajamas, grabbed his rifle and flashlight and ran outside. He was too late to see the predator, but he did scare him away. He was also too late for one of the chickens, or so we thought.

Our chain-link chicken pen was probably twenty yards from the house, not far from the outdoor kitchen building. The pen was in two sections. We kept chickens on one side while grass grew on the other, and then we transferred the chickens and planted grass on the first side. From time to time, leopards and other wild animals still roamed freely through our mission compound. On this night, a leopard or another animal somehow had penetrated the pen.

The chicken we thought was dead began moving. Dad picked her up and saw a deep, ragged gash in her side. He brought her inside the house and proceeded to "doctor" her by filling the wound with sulfa powder and stitching it up with Mom's nylon sewing thread. The chicken miraculously

so many hats!

recovered and lived a happy life with the other bantams — until her turn in the stew pot.

This event was one of those little things God allowed to happen for a reason. Not long after this, one of the Bampende men, harvesting some palm nuts, fell out of the tree. He landed on the sharp, serrated edge of a palm branch on the ground, which cut deeply into his neck, just missing the jugular vein. His friends brought him to Dad, the *"mundele ya Nzambi"* (white man of God). Dad had a reputation in the area of being able to "fix" anything.

Guess what Dad remembered? Yes, the chicken! He did the same thing with the man I'll call Mulongo. Dad cleaned the wound, stuffed it with sulfa powder and sewed it shut with nylon thread. Dad then took him in the car to the Idiofa government clinic, about an hour's drive away. There a doctor took over Mulongo's care, telling Dad that he had done the right thing and probably saved Mulongo's life. *But we knew Who had actually wanted this man's life saved and Who had given Dad some hands-on training for it with the wounded chicken! I wish I knew what became of Mulongo. I hope he learned that he could be a "muntu ya Nzambi" (person of God).*

The African oil palms that were so prevalent in our area were a great source of food and oil (see "Twenty Uses for a Palm Tree," chapter 20). But harvesting the fruit from a tall, mature tree could be dangerous. Jagged, sharp stalks where the branches had been cut off covered the lower part of the tree. The African "walked" his way up the trunk with a loose belt around himself and the tree. He cut the cluster of palm nuts with his machete and then descended. The procedure was a risky business, as Mulongo demonstrated.

17.

Problem Solving – Congo Style

Having a vegetable garden was necessary for us. Our soil was sandy and poor, but because we raised chickens and goats, fertilizer was readily available. We hauled water in 55-gallon barrels from the river by car and then distributed it to the growing plants by bucket or watering can. Congo has no cold weather – only hot weather year-round. It has two seasons – "rainy" and "dry." We could plant any time, but in the rainy season we had to haul less water. So, in Mom's letter to her parents written on December 31, 1951, it is no surprise that she starts out by telling them that we were enjoying fresh corn from the garden for our New Year's meal!

Our local people successfully grew corn, yams, peanuts, manioc and gourds. They raised chickens, pigs and goats, but they often used these animals for monetary exchange, bridal dowry, etc., and only occasionally slaughtered them for meat. Protein was scarce, and any source of wild meat was a treat for them. So whenever we traveled, Dad took his rifle so he could shoot birds or monkeys for the village people to boost their protein intake.

About one of our trips Mom wrote: "We were traveling along and saw something in the road and realized it was a monkey. He was hopping up and down and running back and forth. Ira grabbed his gun but before he could shoot, the monkey ran up a tree where there was a troop of them. Ira shot the biggest one, but it didn't fall. So he shot it again and then realized it was dead but caught on a limb. He also shot a smaller one. Then we tried to figure out how to get the big monkey down from the thirty-foot tree. We tried throwing things to dislodge it and then tried shooting to shatter the branch holding it. But neither worked. We even tried climbing the tree but couldn't get near enough. We took the small monkey and started on but felt badly because the natives are so hungry for meat.

"A few miles down the road, we met a native and asked if he could get the monkey down for us. We drove him back and enjoyed watching him figure out a solution. He borrowed our machete and cut down a small twelve-foot tree and leaned it against the tall tree. Then he cut a long forked stick and fastened that to a pole. From another tree he obtained bark to make string and tied that to the pole. He shimmied up the leaning tree to the first branch, pulling his pole up by the string he had attached to it. Then he climbed from one branch to another until he was near the monkey. Once he reached the upper branch, *he stood up!* With the hook on the end of the pole, he pulled the monkey down. We gave him ten cents [a day's pay in Congo at that time], a pheasant Ira had shot earlier in the day, and a Gospel of Luke in his language."

Raising corn or getting a dead monkey down from a tree Congo-style are problems that can be solve with time, energy and creativity: Sin in our lives is a problem that can only be solved in a God-style way. We cannot solve it by things we do. God, in His mercy, has made provision for the solution to sin in the world – He sent His Son, Jesus, to take the penalty for sin on Himself by dying for us. *"Not by works of righteousness which we have done, but according to His mercy He saved us..." (Titus 3:5)*. Our part is simple: We don't have to figure it out. We just have to believe. As Acts 16:31 says, *"Believe on the Lord Jesus Christ, and you will be saved."*

18.

Hazards of a Congo Picnic

One thing I have always admired about my parents was their zest for life. For the sake of doing something fun, they would venture into unknown dangers. They saw humor in interesting situations. Mom was especially good at finding a bottom line or moral when she described things in her journals or letters to family in the States.

The Belgian government had designated certain days as legal holidays when businesses and schools could close. One time in 1951 while I was away at boarding school, Mom and Dad decided on one of those holidays, with no school or workmen on the station, to pack a picnic lunch and go on a hike. They started by walking into the forest at a location where they had never been before.

They enjoyed the coolness of the forest shade and the refreshing sounds of a small stream. What a treat to get away from the noises of the mission – school children chanting, workmen chopping wood or children crying. They enjoyed the hike until Dad stumbled into carnivorous soldier ants. He was able to warn Mom, who circumvented them. Then they accidentally disturbed a wasp's nest, and Dad got a sting that made him temporarily sick. After that, Mom, walking along the trail, barely missed stepping on a poisonous snake. Dad, in the rear at that time, saw it slither away from her. They didn't say what kind of poisonous snake it was, but we had black mambas in that area, and a bite from one of them could be fatal in minutes.

Mom wrote in her journal that night how, on their trek home, she thought that all the bad things had missed her. But by the time they got home, she had a stiff, swollen thumb. Something had bitten her. She never mentioned the picnic lunch. I wonder, did they eat it by the stream? Or did they abort their hike and eat at home? Mom never said.

So many times in the course of their four years in that part of Congo, God protected my parents from serious harm. *Proverbs 2:8 assures us that the Lord protects the walk of His faithful ones.*

Congo had plenty of creatures that were to be feared. We saw tarantulas, scorpions (Mom was bitten once), and snakes. Mosquitoes and tsetse flies were a threat to our health. Wasps or yellow jackets frequently stung Dad. Then there were the invisible threats – the amoebas that caused dysentery, hookworms, or flies that carried filaria (the disease that leads to elephantiasis). Thankfully, most of these were treatable.

19.

Chief Masud Comes to Church

    I wish Mom had written more about the chiefs in our area of Congo. I have color pictures of four of them in full regalia but with no names attached. The chiefs I remember from our nearby villages of Mangungu and Luembe were friendly and accepting of us. They made sure the children of their villages attended school, and they encouraged the village people to come to church. To my knowledge, none of the chiefs personally accepted Christ while we were there.

    In an August 1950 letter, Dad wrote about Chief Masud of Mangungu: "Three Sundays ago, the chief from Mangungu brought every man, woman and child in his section to church, making about one hundred in addition to our regular two hundred; so we had a full house. He has been there now three Sundays in a row. The first Sunday he sat and played with his bracelets and skirt, yawned and burped loudly. I don't think he heard a thing I said, but the second week he was very attentive. The third Sunday he brought others. Now he sits in the front row and seldom takes his eyes off me. Pray for Masud that he will accept Christ as his Chief and make a public profession."

    Chief Mbengemundele (means "white man's money") attended church one of the first Sundays Dad tried to preach in *Kikongo* and was struggling with the words. Chief Mbengemundele got up and "preached." He was an unbeliever but apparently had attended church enough in the past to know what Dad was trying to say!

Then there was Chief Mukwese from Luembe Village – very helpful and congenial. In the spring of 1950, he attended church a few times. Then one Sunday, Chief Mukwese was absent but sent a letter with a village boy saying that he was in a village near Mingontsi and had cut his leg badly coming down a hill on his bicycle, and he could not return to Luembe. In the letter he asked Dad to come get him in the car.

Mom wrote about that trip: "It was a nice sunny day; so we started out in Woody with four of our Christian school boys to get him. We had not eaten lunch yet, and thinking it was but a few miles, we took only a bottle of water and a six-inch square piece of leftover cake with us. The chief's location turned out to be sixty-five miles away. So part way there, we shared the cake with the boys. When we arrived at Mingontsi, it was raining lightly, and by the time we had located Chief Mukwese and started back, it was raining a real downpour.

"All the way going we sang hymns and talked of spiritual things with the boys. They are very receptive in such an informal setting. On the return trip, things were a little tenser with the rain pouring down and the non-believing chief in the car. By the time we reached the ferry, about fifteen miles from home, the roads were really slick. Out on the prairie, the land is all sand, and rain helps, but such is not the case near the rivers where there is red clay soil. This soil is solid and good except during a rain."

Dad continued the saga: "Well, to make the story short and get to the best part, we slid onto the ferry and off on the other side and then started to ascend the hill. But we could only get about half way up. Our wheels were not getting traction; so Carol and the boys got out and pushed, but we only gained a few feet. The ferrymen joined us and helped push, and we finally reached the brow of the hill. The ferrymen advised us to wait until the rain stopped to go further, because ahead of us foot-deep water was washing over the sandy section of the road. Then there was another clay hill past that with about three more miles of climbing. We were all soaked, hungry and thirsty and didn't want to wait or spend the night there. So with a short prayer for God's help, we started out. It was three miles of winding, twenty-degree upgrade, slippery clay all the way. We began and stayed in second gear for fear we would lose the slight traction we were getting. Only the crown between the tracks and the Lord's hand kept us from slipping into the ditch on either side. Wheels spinning all the way, we finally broke over the top of the hill, and the boys spontaneously broke into hymns of praise and thanksgiving to the Lord. They sang '*Kiese Mingi*' (Running Over) and then without a break 'Every Day, Every Hour' (in *Kikongo*)."

I would love to know the rest of the story about these chiefs who were such an important part of our Congo experience. I hope the seed planted in those days took root, and they became believers along with their families. I hope to meet all of these chiefs in Heaven.

***Mom discovered the hind section
of a rat in her bowl***

20.

Beware the Village Stew!

What would missionary stories be without descriptions of traditional native gourmet foods? If I were to make up a menu card listing some of the delicious items we experienced in the Belgian Congo in the late forties and early fifties, it might read like this:

Flying Ants (off the wing)
Chunky Rat Stew
Bowl of Boiled Fish Eyes
Shish Kebab Grasshoppers
Rolled Grubs in Banana Leaves
"Luku" (manioc root porridge)
"Sukasuk" (manioc leaf pureed spinach)
Monkey Meat Stew

My father, mother and I (between the three of us) experienced all of the above. I was the only one, however, to brave the flying ants. When the ants were in season, the African children taught me how to catch them on the wing. We held them by the wings and then bit off the body, flicking away the wings.

My parents experienced the rat stew when the chief invited them to supper in a neighboring village. They were all seated around the fire pit in the village courtyard and were dished up bowls of stew. Mom had the misfortune of discovering an entire hind section of a rat, including hair and tail, in her bowl.

It was Dad who was served the most valued dish when he was on a hunting trip with some of the tribal Christians. The group stayed the night in a village and were hospitably offered supper. The Africans all received bowls of fish stew, but Dad (the only white man) was given preferential treatment and handed a bowl full of fish eyes. It was also Dad who dared to taste the roasted grasshoppers and grubs.

We all ate *luku* and *sukasuk* when dining in the villages. These dishes were the staple diet of the lower Congo peoples. Luku was made from the root of the manioc plant. Naturally toxic, it was first soaked in the swamp for a period and then dried on roofs before being pounded into flour and boiled into a thick porridge. This was scooped up with the fingers and dipped into the spinach.

My boarding school served monkey meat stew as often as the cook was able to buy monkeys from the local hunters. It tasted better before I knew what it was. Food is definitely a part of the cultural experience of missionaries and – praise God – covered by His grace!

21.

Twenty Uses for a Palm Tree

The palm trees we had in Congo were "Red Oil African Palms" (*Elgeis quineensis*). They are beautiful and majestic, standing tall, branches exploding from a central core with fronds dangling in delicate symmetry. We had fifty of them on our Mangungu compound. The following are some of the uses we knew for the palms:

1. Landscaping
2. Shade
3. Siding – The fronds were woven together to make a mat called *mandala* that would be used for the outer walls of their houses.
4. Roof poles were made from the hardy spines.
5. String (raffia) was made from the fronds.
6. Heavier string was woven from the trunk fibers.
7. Palm nuts were eaten. They were a shiny orange fruit about the size of a walnut. We boiled the nuts in salted water, chewed them until all the orange oil was gone and then spit out the fibers and kernel.
8. Cooking oil

9. Oil from the palm nuts was used cosmetically as a lubricant for the skin or hair.
10. Oil was also used in commercial manufacturing (example: Palm-olive soap)[6]
11. Palm nut center (a nut about the size of a hazelnut) was also edible.
12. Fertilizer was made from the rotten trees.
13-19. Seven dietary supplements are derived from the oil palm nut: nutritional helps for cardiovascular health, Alzheimer's, arthritis, asthma, cataracts, high blood pressure and macular degeneration.

Mom didn't know about any of the dietary supplements, but on October 12, 1949, she wrote to her sister in the States: "We thought we knew about all the possible uses for the red oil palm tree, but we were mistaken. Ira bought two trees from a nearby village for sixteen cents each to use on our station. Our workmen cut them down and hauled them to us. But we later heard from our workmen that the tree cutting had caused a big *palaver*. The villagers were arguing with them over the tree *stumps*! The workmen said the stumps belonged to them because their white man had bought the trees. The villagers claimed the stumps were still in the village so they belonged to the village. In the end (Mom wrote), the workmen won." What was the reason for the intense argument? *The delicious grubs in the stumps!* And that's use number 20.

We have seen at least twenty ways that man uses the red oil palm. When my husband and I were discussing this after reading Mom's letter and researching the medicinal uses of the red palm, we got to thinking about how many ways we could be used by God. Have you ever thought about listing what you could do for — or give back — to God? I think the

---

[6] A palm oil factory run by the Lever Brothers with a large ex-patriot staff was near us at Leverville.

number would be bigger than twenty! You might make it a "bucket list" of ways you could be useful to God. And then you could do them!

We read in Philippians 4:13: *"I can do all things through Christ who strengthens me."*

22.

Mom's "Cliff Hangers"

*I*n reading through Mom's journals of happenings in the Belgian Congo, I noticed how often she wrote at length about something and then ended her entry with an intriguing last line without further explanation. For example, after describing in detail a day in our first trip across Congo in 1948, she ended the journaling with this statement: *"Found a snake in my shoe."* My question is *"and then what?"*

Several days later in the journal entries about the same trip, she closed with *"We heard a leopard in the night."* That's all? The first time any of us had ever heard a leopard in the night, and that's all she said?

During their early days at Mangungu, Mom described a huge *palaver* she and Dad had with the chief and village people after some of the children were caught breaking into the schoolhouse and stealing. How did Mom end that story? She ended with this phrase: *"They point with their tongues."* As near as I could tell, that had nothing to do with the story, but it was an interesting fact about the Congolese people. They did point with their tongues to indicate direction. Perhaps the kids were "pointing" to the guilty ones.

so many hats!

Here is another of Mom's cliff hangers: *"The Brower boys are a handful."* This statement stood alone in a journal entry about a trip we took to the mission headquarters at Tshene, about a day's travel from Mangungu. Perhaps the Arthur Brower family (also with our mission) was there, but Mom didn't mention it. I agree with Mom that the Brower boys were a handful. There were four tow headed boys. One time when they visited us at Mangungu, the boys smashed my entire collection of ceramic miniatures.

In a letter to her parents, Mom inserted this sentence in the middle of a paragraph about something else entirely: *"A cat is on the ceiling, and dirt is falling on me."* I know how that could be, but did her parents? Our house was mud block with a grass roof, and the ceilings were bamboo woven mats stretched across the tops of the walls. Animals could get under the eaves fairly easily. In fact, creatures often scampered across the ceilings – mice most often. Even a huge snake once!

In another letter, Mom told about making my birthday cake and about Dad building a playhouse for me in the backyard. It was a tiny, one-room structure made with banana leaves. It had a grass roof, a door and a window. To end the paragraph about my birthday, she wrote: *"We butchered and canned a pig on Tuesday."* Yuck, Mom.

Mom described our church services at Mangungu – how the church could seat 300 people and usually had more than 100 for Sunday morning worship. She explained that a hollowed-out log drum in the back of the building called the villagers to the service. She described the building as an open structure with a roof and half-walls. Then she said, *"We sat on the front bench, and it broke."* What she didn't explain was that the church benches were made of forked sticks with crosspieces and connected by long bamboo poles to form the seats. Women sat on one side of the church and men on the other. We commonly heard the crack and then the squeals of the women when a bench broke. By 1950, Dad had replaced most of the bamboo benches with long boards. Chickens still ran through the church building, but at least the distraction of broken benches was eliminated.

23.

Last Flight

I'm talking about the last flight of Sabena Airlines DC-3 identity number 00-CBN, en route from Costermansville (Bukavu) to Leopoldville (Kinshasa) in the Belgian Congo on February 4, 1952. Sixteen people were on board – twelve passengers including three children plus four crew members. All were European except for one Congolese, a steward. This was the last scheduled flight for the Belgian pilot before his retirement. In fact, this was his last flight, period. The flight ended abruptly at 1 p.m. three miles from the Congo Gospel Mission station of Mangungu-Luembe and only three-fourths of the way to the plane's destination.

On the mission station it was siesta time, and we three Crosses were resting when we heard the sound of a plane overhead that was having engine failure. Dad rushed outside in time to see the DC-3 pull into a vertical climb and then fall off into a nosedive, dropping out of sight over the nearest ridge. A second later, a huge cloud of black smoke poured into the air. We jumped into our car and arrived at the crash site less than ten minutes after the plane went down. We had to park and walk to reach the site. As we broke through the prairie grass, we viewed a scene that we found impossible to grasp – a huge area flattened by the crash and strewn with debris. The fuel had burned itself out, and only the big tires were still sending up black smoke. Bodies were scattered over the entire area.

Villagers from nearby had arrived ahead of us and kept crying, "They are all dead! They are all dead!" This is when Mom sent me to wait in the car.

The saga continues in a letter by Dad: "We ran quickly to all the bodies, and only when I was sure that no one was left alive, I took a few quick pictures of the site. Leaving several responsible Christian natives on guard (papers and money were scattered all over), we started for Idiofa to get the officials. On the way we met a Catholic priest on his motorcycle. He offered to go to Idiofa to get the officials while we returned to the crash site to wait. We didn't touch anything until the officials got there and then were able to assist them by picking up the papers, money, etc. We helped lay out the bodies to wait for truck transport to Idiofa where funerals were held later."

Dad continued: "The next day engineers and state investigators were here from Kikwit, Leopoldville and Belgium. The investigators have questioned us minutely for hours at a time. The brunt of testimony has been on us. After all this, the investigators left with the mystery of the plane's crash still unresolved."

But, in the forest a few miles away lay a propeller from the plane. Local villagers knew about its location, but they didn't tell. They saw my Dad, "their white man" at the crash. They saw that the Sabena officials gave Dad everything that was left of the plane (stuff he was able to use for building projects, repairs, etc.), and they, in their superstitious way of thinking, thought Dad must have brought the plane down with his "magic." They said they had tried to bring planes down, but it never worked. They didn't want to get Dad in trouble; so they waited until after the investigators had

Last Flight

gone to tell him. As soon as he learned of the propeller, he again contacted the officials, who returned and examined the missing propeller. That was all they needed to confirm the cause of the crash. They read the clues by the scratch marks on the propeller!

In 2016 we were able to uncover the details of the crash in an online archive. The report listed the cause of the crash as follows: "The control cables in the fuselage were sheared by the right propeller, which had been projected following a shaft failure caused by the sudden stopping of the engine caused by fatigue failure of No. 6 piston lug." Dad always put it more simply. He said: "The engine jammed, causing the propeller to twist off and cut through the cables to the rear of the plane so the pilot had no control."

However you put it, the result was the same. It was the last flight for that plane. In ten seconds, the lives and futures of the sixteen people on board Sabena 00-CBN on February 4, 1952, were ended. It was their last flight. How many of them were saved and will be in Heaven? We do not know. Nor do we know when we will experience the last ten seconds of our lives.

Are we ready for our "last flight"? Second Corinthians 6:2b says: *"Now is the day of salvation."* How can we receive that salvation? By recognizing we are sinners and that Jesus died to take our penalty for sin. In Romans 10:9 we read: *"If you confess with your mouth Jesus as Lord, and believe in your heart that God raised Him from the dead, you shall be saved."* **And you will be ready for that "last flight."**

*Our mail carrier walked 25 miles to Idiofa
for the mail each week*

24.

Here Comes the Mailman!

We received mail once a week. The mail carrier left Mangungu at the first crowing of the rooster, usually about 3 a.m. He walked the twenty-five miles to Idiofa, the nearest government post. There he dropped off any outgoing letters, picked up the mail bag for us and then walked the twenty-five miles back to Mangungu, usually arriving at dusk. He did this for thirteen cents!

Mail day was always exciting. Letters from family and friends were our only connection with the United States. We were isolated from the outside world because we had no radio communication, no television, no computers and no newspapers. Mom and Dad's support ($125 per month) came three times a year. Out of it they paid the workmen and schoolteachers, paid their own living expenses, bought gasoline and the school kids' clothes – and more!

If a package arrived at the post in Idiofa, the carrier had to bring a slip for Mom and Dad to sign, and then he returned the next day to pick up the package. Getting packages was so special. Mom's parents frequently sent boxes with items we had requested and included treats of their choosing. This is how we received some of the essential things, such as garden seeds, baking powder, yeast, cake mixes, root beer extract (we made our own root beer) and most important, Hershey bars!

To our knowledge, we received every package sent. The Belgian Congo government had a system of checks and balances on packages. In Leopoldville, the capital city, a government worker assigned each package a number, and a numbered tag accompanied the package to its outpost. The tag had to be signed and returned to Leopoldville. Mom wrote that even though we never missed a package, "hands sometimes got into the package" if it was poorly sealed. All our packages came by boat mail and took up to four months to arrive.

Dad wrote about one time when he and Mom were returning from a trip to Kikwit for supplies. They came to a truck stuck in the sand. Dad helped the driver dig the truck out and then offered a ride to the soldier who was a passenger in the truck. He was delivering the mail to Idiofa. The truck driver was drunk and belligerent and refused to allow Dad to drive ahead of him. The soldier told Dad they had already been stuck six times earlier. And sure enough, Mom and Dad came upon the driver later – again stuck in the sand! This time Dad left him stuck there and continued to Idiofa with the soldier, got our mail and returned home.

Mom wrote in a letter to her parents on October 8, 1949, about a special package they had received that included "birthday party" things for my birthday. To start the celebration, the Angus Browers with their four children from Kifwanzondo came for a fried chicken supper. Mom wrote to her parents: "Margie's birthday was a success. We made paper hats and streamers with the crepe paper you sent and made the room look like a party. After supper each person un-wrapped a gift that had been tied on the end of a streamer – things you had sent – everything from shoe strings to toy airplanes. We played a couple games and then gave Margie her presents. About the View-Master you sent for her, she said, 'Now I have my own and can look at the pictures anytime I want.'" I remember letting the African kids look at the pictures through it. The 3-D idea was incomprehensible to them, and they kept feeling the space behind it, trying to figure out how those things got there!

Christmas packages were a treat for us, even if they didn't arrive until February. My parents read word-for-word any newspaper used for packing in the boxes, so starved they were for reading material. And Mom carefully saved every scrap of wrapping paper and ribbon for use the following year. After we had set up our Christmas tree in 1951, Mom wrote: "We decorated a tree branch in our living room and put the wrapped gifts under it. The decorations looked so festive that they made our curtains look shabby. So I made new ones." Christmas was when we gave each of the school kids a set of new clothes. And at the church service we gave each attendee a bit of rock salt.

Toward the end of our term in July of 1951, Mom wrote to family: "For three weeks our mail hasn't been worth mentioning – some ads and a business letter. Guess it's about time for furlough; everyone seems to have forgotten us completely. Three times we have sent the mail boy the twenty-five miles to Idiofa on foot, and he returned with an empty sack saying that he walked '*mpamba*' (for nothing). English has no word like *mpamba* – it can mean empty, void, zero or useless."

The telegram (also coming through Idiofa) telling Mom that her Dad had passed away arrived ten days after being sent! Then a few months later, just before we left on furlough, another telegram (more timely this time) arrived, announcing her mother's death. Now, in the age of e-mail, cell phones, texting, Skype, Face book, Twitter and Tweet, communication is so instant that it is hard to imagine waiting weeks to receive a letter. Communication was one of the challenges missionaries faced in the early days. Missionaries today face different ones. But they all faced, and still face, the same challenge of learning to communicate with the people in order to tell the lost about the saving grace of Jesus.

Dad made a washing machine in 1951 out of a 55-gallon steel drum. A shaft ran through the length of it with wooden paddles on the inside and a crank handle on the outside. This washing machine sat on top of a stone fire pit where a fire heated the water. The laundry boy cranked the handle. Voila, clean clothes!

25.

Our New Stone House

Our mud block house with grass roof, bamboo-mat ceilings, river clay-plastered walls and rough cement floor had well served the Hallers at Mangungu for more than sixteen years. And it had served us for two years, but it was "falling down around our ears," as Dad put it. Rats and termites had eaten out the mud walls, causing part of one wall to collapse. The mat ceilings sagged, and the roof leaked.

So, Dad, between other pressing mission jobs, designed a 30 by 50 foot floor plan (two-bedroom, one bath, dining room, living room, kitchen, storeroom, office, and open entry porch to the kitchen). He hired workmen and school kids to carry rock and sand from the river. He would use the rock for the outside walls. The inside walls would be poured cement. Excerpts from Mom's journals chronicle the actual building progress:

"Today (September 16, 1950), we had to stop work on our house and build some benches for the church. The old bamboo ones keep breaking, so we are making more permanent benches out of twelve foot long mahogany boards. These cost about forty cents each. The bonus is that because this is a Congo wood, the termites don't eat it."

She continued (December, 1950): "The school girls are coming with rocks on their heads for the new house. They carry four for one cent, but we pay them in clothes. [For each school child, Mom kept a card that she would punch with each delivery.] When they have earned thirty cents, they get a dress. We recently got a real buy in a local market – boys' shirts for thirty two cents each! We bought fifty of them to have for pay for the boys."

In July of 1951 she wrote: "The walls are up halfway to the windows.... The window frames are in.... Foot-high weeds are growing in the dirt floors.... We took a break to build a fence around the church building to keep out the goats that have decided to take up residence there.... Schoolboys are breaking up rocks for gravel for the inside walls.... Ira is making plans for the fireplace from a design in the encyclopedia.... We are ready to put the grass roof on...."

"A big work saver," she wrote, "has been a saw with a motor. A neighboring missionary gave us a saw, and Ira is rigging it up to his motorcycle engine. With this to rip boards, the work on the house will go quicker. The workers are now carrying poles and grass for the roof. We also just finished re-roofing the church."

November 22, 1951, Mom wrote: "We are working hard to finish our house and get into it by Christmas. We are now framing screens for the windows and have eight out of seventeen done. Ira is putting up beautiful rosewood ceilings. The work is slow because the boards are hand-sawn and have to be wedged, trimmed, and sanded, etc. to fit together. Margie's room is plastered and ready for paint."

That was Mom's last entry about the house.

Note by Margie in 2016: I honestly do not remember if we got into the new house by Christmas or not, but I do remember living briefly in it before leaving for furlough. My room had Venetian blinds that my grandparents had sent, and the room had a real closet. My memories of the house include helping Mom buy eggs from the village women on the little back porch.

We never lived in the house again except for a few weeks almost three years later. Congo Gospel Mission dissolved while we were stateside, so we were unable to return to work at Mangungu. CGM gave that property over to the Baptist Mid-Missions. For reasons unknown to me, BMM did not accept my parents' application to return to Congo with them. We were only able to stop by to retrieve our stored household goods for the move to the Kivu Province to work with the Berean Mission. Part II of this book covers that period of our Congo experiences.

You might be wondering about the workers, including children, who helped carry the materials for building the stone house. Their work might sound like child slave labor, but in that culture at that time, they did the work willingly. The villages were so poor that they embraced the opportunity to earn mere pennies or clothing or rock salt. Such work was the way the children paid for their schooling, schoolbooks and clothes. For the workmen, it was a way to provide for their families. The wages were competitive with the government ones. Missionaries had house staff, not only freeing up their time for mission work, but also giving opportunity for the local people to earn a little extra money.

Often in her letters to family and praying friends, Mom thanked them for their part (by giving and praying), thus making it possible for us to be in Congo. My parents loved the Congolese and met the challenges of pioneer missionary work head-on, counting it a privilege to be there. The next chapter, "Bearing Fruit," expresses that.

Women bringing their "mambus" to Mom

26.

Bearing Fruit

"*Holding forth the Word of Life that I [we] may rejoice in the day of Christ*" (Philippians 2:16 KJV). Ira and Carol Cross chose this as the theme verse for their time in Congo.

In describing the work of "holding forth the Word" at Mangungu station, Mom wrote on May 20, 1950: "School started last week with 147 registrants. I have classes until noon and then a couple more in the afternoon. We have six teacher-monitors in the station and village schools. I make out all the lessons, correct the papers, give exams, lead the choir, and teach the six daily Bible classes as well.

"This week has been a real blessing, and we feel the Lord working. For example, the chief of Mangungu village came to chapel for the first time. The next Sunday we had a large group from his village, and then Wednesday night for prayer meeting we had many women from the village. The church was full; so we decided to have a testimony time. Afterward, we could hardly stop the praying but did so because the children were getting tired.

"On Thursday, forty-seven women arrived for Bible class. This time, though, they really listened!" The most Mom ever had in the women's class was ninety. Mom often mentioned how hard the women's ministry was for her. She felt her teaching fell on deaf ears. But she had a special way of connecting with the women when they came to her for help. They would come to the verandah and "cough" to announce their presence. Then they would explain about the *mambu* (problem) and get her wisdom.

She continued in her letter: "Last night we played the phonograph on the verandah, and the children came to listen to Bible stories and music. Then we had a singing time with Ira playing the guitar.

"With all this increased interest in spiritual things, we are planning to organize teams with Christian young men to go into the villages after the Sunday services."

Then Dad wrote to family in America: "Twenty-seven have professed salvation in the two years we have been here and seem to be living changed lives.... We are planning our first baptismal service soon. A year ago, Margie came forward in a church service of her own free will and gave her testimony in *Kikongo* of her saving faith in Jesus. I am hoping that she will be my first baptism.

"We went to another village meeting this week led by Kinende, one of our first believers. After his message, we sang 'All for Jesus.' Oh, how we love these people here at Mangungu.... We are homesick for the upcoming furlough, but just last Sunday when four more accepted the Lord, it made us not want to leave and miss the joy of leading more to Christ."

Mom and Dad's ministry was not about numbers, although the numbers were encouraging. Whether they taught school, preached, built buildings, treated ulcers, or pulled teeth, they did it all for Jesus. *This is what I saw in my parents in the Belgian Congo.*

There were ten of us baptized on June 24, 1951, Dad's first baptismal service was held in a little river about a mile away down our main Idiofa road. After the church service, we all walked down the hill, singing hymns. I was the first one baptized. We closed the baptismal service by singing "Shall We Gather at the River?" A second baptismal service for six young men was held on October 14, 1951.

Part 1 –
Kwilu District Photographs

Ira, Margie and Carol Cross

"For whosoever shall call upon the name of the Lord shall be saved.

"How then shall they call on him in whom they have not believed? and how shall they believe in him of whom they have not heard? and how shall they hear without a preacher?

"And how shall they preach, except they be sent? as it is written, How beautiful are the feet of them that preach the gospel of peace, and bring glad tidings of good things!"—Rom. 10:13-15.

Your prayers will speed our feet in carrying God's word to Africa

"The Fields are White Already to Harvest."

THE CONGO GOSPEL MISSION
(A Fundamental Mission of Faith)
215 Villa Ave.   Villa Park, Illinois

Cross family prayer card, 1948

Ira Cross points to the Belgian Congo

Hand-painted sign to our mission station

Water carriers at Mangungu

Bampende women's topknot hairdos

Margie pulling bamboo car

Missionary children's boarding school at Kipungu

1947 "Woody" and 1928 Model A ("Torpedo")

Margie with teacher's baby

Carol and Ira Cross 1950

Mingantsi *Mangungu chief with wife*

Crash of Sabena plane February 4, 1952

Our new stone house at Mangungu, 1952

Mangungu-Luembe church building

First baptism at river, June 24, 1951

Margie after baptism

Part II –
Kivu Province Photographs

Wartime truck in New York before shipping, 1954

Ferry on a river in the Congo

Crosses' two-room leaf house at Uku

Berean Mission Academy Eighth grade graduates, 1956

Margie with Pet baboons, "Jojo" and "Peeps"

PART TWO

In the Kivu Province of Belgian Congo

December 1954 – August 1957

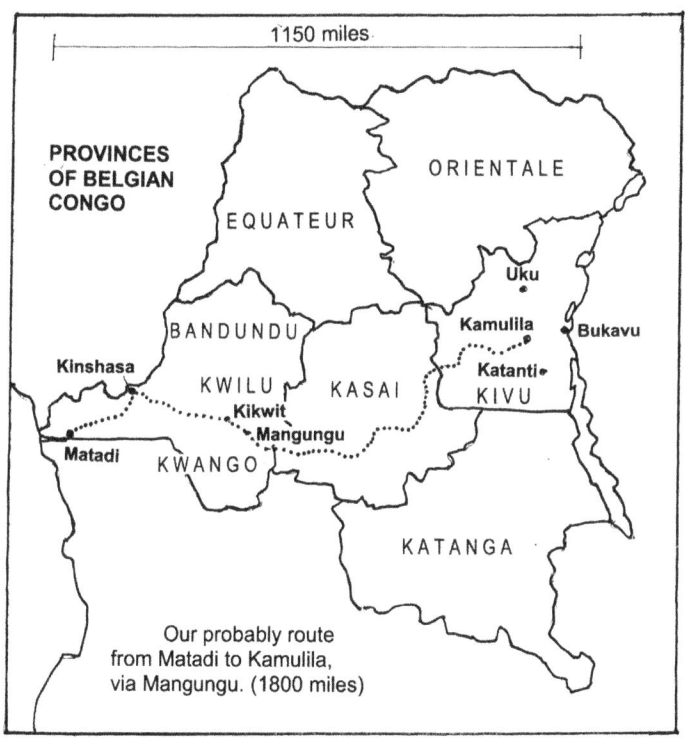

Map of Crosses' trip from Matadi to the Kivu

27.

A Day in the Life of a Truck

    This was not just *any* truck. It was an old war-time truck that Dad shipped, loaded, to Congo in 1954. I could write a book about the truck alone, but this story covers just one almost typical day in its life as we made our way across Congo. We were going from the port city of Matadi to our new post, via our former mission station, Mangungu. We had planned to be there for Christmas, load up our stored belongings, and drive on to the Kivu Province where my parents were to work with the Berean Mission. The Congo Gospel Mission had dissolved, and we were unable to return to that field, but wanting to serve God in Congo, my parents had applied to Berean.

    Dad, ever resourceful, when writing about this particular day, called it "an interesting experience." I would have called it something else! After its lengthy boat trip, the truck was sluggish starting; so Dad bought a new battery for it. That was not, however, the end of its starting problems. It was a hot day, and we took a break to cool off by washing in a stream. Then the old truck wouldn't start. Dad tried to start it by rolling backward downhill, but that didn't work. So he took the starter off.

so many hats!

This is how he described the situation: "The starter spring was almost tied in a knot with part of the gizmo broken so that it bound up and wouldn't turn." Remember, we were in the middle of Congo, primarily traveling on one-lane dirt roads[7] with little or no traffic and definitely *no* services. Dad did something to the starter that allowed it to turn more freely. He also replaced the points and condenser with new ones he had brought along. The truck started!

By now it was suppertime so Mom cooked a camp supper for us. It was getting dark, and we didn't want to spend the night at that spot, so we continued down the road, hoping to find a good pull off and place to camp. After about two hours, we started up a little grade, and everything quit! Dad lit the pressure lantern, popped the hood, and found that the facing had broken off the new contact points. He replaced those with the old ones. By this time, Dad was dead tired and discouraged. Again, the starter stubbornly refused to work.

We rolled backward down the hill enough to get off the road and went to bed with the mosquitoes that ate us alive, even through the covers! The next morning while we were making breakfast, a white man in a Carryall loaded with locals drove by. The white man nodded and drove on but soon came back and stopped. He was a Baptist missionary from about fifteen miles away. He gave us a ride to his station. In discussing the dilemma, he told Dad they had quit using Fords years before, but some old pieces might still be lying around the mission station.

A V-8 motor with a questionable starter lay in the back of the station. Dad quickly installed the starter in our truck. It didn't start. So the missionary pulled us with his pickup, but our truck still wouldn't start. Dad dug into it again and once more, in his "technical" terms, described the mechanical

---

[7] Congo, at this time, had a total of twenty-five miles of paved road in the entire country.

problem this way: "It was all gummed up, and a tiny insulating washer got left off." He fixed that, and the truck finally started. Dad's last comment: "We went on our way, rejoicing over having again seen the Lord place the right man at the right place and time to solve an otherwise impossible situation."

28.

Christmas in Popokebaba

Let me tell you how we ended up spending Christmas of 1954 with five white French-speaking, bearded, bachelor Catholic priests in a remote village in the Belgian Congo. The Christmas celebration wasn't what we had planned, but it was what God had planned for us. We were on our way across Congo (some 1,800 miles) in an old war-issue Ford truck Dad had acquired in California. My parents had been transferred to another part of Congo, and we were driving by our old station of Mangungu to pick up household items we had stored there when we went on furlough. We were a three days' drive from there when our plans got derailed.

The day was December 22. We were trucking along when the engine began emitting warning sounds. Mind you, we were probably 150 miles from any large town where parts *might* be available. Then came a loud bang, and all forward movement ceased. In fact, everything ceased. Dad, a self-taught mechanic, began the process of taking the engine apart and placing the parts in hubcaps and dishpans, etc., under the truck. The final diagnosis was a blown piston. Dad could do nothing more there in the middle of nowhere; so he got his "whizzer" motor bike off the truck bed and left for places unknown to see what he might find. That meant Mom and I were alone with the truck in a remote area where it was highly unlikely that any other vehicle would pass for hours or even days.

Then rain began to fall. Hard. Mom and I sat in the cab and watched water race down the sandy road. Sand was eroding from around the truck tires. So we got out, found the shovel and began digging trenches to control the water runoff. That helped, and two hours later the rain stopped. Because darkness was beginning to fall, we pitched the tent and began camp supper preparations. That was when Dad returned, his bike in the back of a pickup driven by an African chauffeur. Dad had encountered some Africans who directed him to a nearby mission station. There he found the five priests who arranged for the ride back to the truck. And even better, miracle that it was, they had an old 6-cylinder vintage dump truck, abandoned and rusting, that they eventually let Dad have for $90.

We camped that night beside our truck. Then in daylight, Dad put the engine pieces back together, and we limped to the mission on five cylinders. There, Dad immediately dismantled the old dump truck to salvage what parts he could to repair our truck. Meanwhile, Mom and I set up housekeeping in the one-room guesthouse, our every action watched by as many villagers as could cram into the open window. They acted as if they never had seen a white woman and white child before. We set up our cots, folding table and chairs, camp stove and cookware. Whenever I ventured outside, the children wanted to feel my hair.

It appeared that we would be staying at the Catholic mission through Christmas. In an attempt to make the holiday festive, we found a branch outside so we would have a Christmas tree and I made paper decorations for it out of scraps of paper. Mom had packed some things for gifts that we wrapped and put under the tree. In the end, our stay lasted two weeks.

Because Christmas Day fell while we were there, the priests took pity on us and invited us to eat Christmas dinner with them. What a blessing that turned out to be – not for the meal itself or even the fellowship, but, as Mom put it in her journal, because of the *ice water*. It was hot, and because we had been camping, we had no refrigeration. Ice was a treat! The priests even served a steamed pudding for dessert. December 25 was Mom's birthday; so she claimed the pudding was her birthday cake!

Around that table the Christmas story was told again – the wonderful story we know so well. How God sent His Son Jesus to be born and eventually die in our place to take our punishment for sin. God did this because He loved us so much. We talked about this around that table.

Ah, yes, that table. It was, or so it seemed to me, to be about the size of a ping-pong table, covered with a once-white sheet, stained and spotted. Flies and ants shared the table. "The food," Mom wrote, "was simple but good, and the ice water *wonderful!*" The Catholic priests had made Christmas special for us.

---

* In those days in Congo, little love was lost between Protestant and Catholic mission workers. They competed seriously to get village children to attend their respective schools. I am not endorsing this attitude, just stating how it was. This competition is what made accepting the Catholic hospitality difficult for my parents, yet they couldn't help but see how God had made this provision in their time of need.

Christmas in the Catholic guest house

29.

New Year's at Mangungu

After celebrating Christmas with five Catholic priests when our truck broke down on the way from Matadi, we finally arrived at Mangungu at one minute after midnight on New Year's Eve. "There's our sign!" one of us exclaimed as our headlights illuminated the hand-painted sign Dad had made during our last term. It stood on a new post but plainly marked the driveway to "Mangungu-Luembe." We slowed down, and Dad swung the truck wide to make the sharp right-angle turn.

Our hearts pounded and our eyes strained through the dark to get the first glimpse of our stone house. The church was still standing, as was the school and our house. The headlights were soon shining on the sentry house. Mandangi, dad's right-hand man who had stayed on the station to keep watch, crawled through their low door first, then his wife, and one by one, his seven children.

We had barely greeted them when other local people gathered. We exchanged many tearful *mbote mingis (greetings)*, accompanied by the tribal "thumb" handshakes. After this touching welcome, we finally said goodnight and entered our house. We walked from room to room, pushing aside spider webs and dust, but found things just as we had left them almost three years prior. We saw no bugs or rats, and everything was dry. Even Dad's guitar, wrapped only in a quilt, was fine. It felt like home. We went to bed at 3 a.m.

We woke up early on New Year's Day and spent most of the day saying *mbote* (hello) to one person after another. Seven of the village chiefs came with school kids who marched and sang for us. Sunday, January 2, the church was packed.

After Dad preached in *Kikongo*, he told the people we were only to be there for a few weeks. We had written this to them from the States, but they didn't want to accept it. Their response was a letter sent to "the church in America" in care of my parents while they were in California. Translated, it read: "*Greetings much much in the name of Jesus Christ. We have heard that you are not returning the Crosses to us. What is the problem? We have judged this, and from the time Crosses came until they went to America, they did no wrong. They say if they come, they will go someplace else. What affair is this? You cut this again and send them back right away. We are finished. The Church of Mangungu-Luembe.*"

After church, the village chiefs and church leaders met to make a plan to keep us there. They decided to refuse to let Mid-Missions have the land. The Mangungu people said they didn't want anyone else, and they had letters for us from villages in the area stating the same thing. Mom wrote in her journal: "This is all terribly hard, but our hands are tied. It is a heart-ache, and one we cannot understand."

Mom went on to write about some sweet fellowship they had while there: "Last night we sat around a campfire with Mandangi and his family of seven children. In the past, we would have roasted peanuts, but for fun we popped corn, something new to them." (*We always had a lot of popcorn because Mom and Dad filled all the loose spaces in our shipping drums with popcorn kernels.*)

New Year's at Mangungu

Note by Margie: Mandangi was Dad's right-hand workman and a fine Christian brother. Dad truly grieved over having to leave these people to whom he had given his heart. The book "We Two Alone" describes the tragic killing of missionary Irene Ferrell at Mangungu in 1964 while her ministry partner, Ruth Hege (author of the book), was spared and protected by some of the Christians on the mission. One of the persons who helped her, according to a note by Mom, was a son of Mandangi. The church building and our stone house were burned by the rebels in 1964, however, the stone walls are still standing.

30.

When the Jungle Ferry Broke Loose

After we spent New Year's 1955 at Mangungu in the Kwilu District of Congo, but before we arrived at Kamulila in the Kivu Province of east Congo (more than 1,300 miles of dirt roads distant), we took an unplanned detour downriver. Our truck was fully loaded with four tons of stuff we had brought with us from the States and picked up at our old station of Mangungu. We were moving to the new area where my parents were assigned. I'm not sure what all the "stuff" was, except I know it included my grandpa's old upright piano, a generator, many barrels and crates of household things, Mom's treadle sewing machine, several drums of gasoline, Daddy's motorbike and much more!

Congo had many rivers and few bridges; so travelers crossed rivers by ferries. Mom recorded in her journal that we crossed at least twenty rivers by ferry on this trip. The ferries generally were wood or metal canoes, somehow tied together, with planks lying across them for cars to drive onto. Additional planks were used as ramps for the boarding and disembarking processes. These planks were rough boards, little wider than the wheels of the vehicles and were usually wet and slippery. The African rowers paddled the ferries across or poled them if the river was shallow enough. Usually the ferry was tethered to a steel cable stretched across the river to prevent the ferry from going downstream. If this all sounds very un-technical, it's because I was a child and not concerned with mechanical details.

I *was,* however, concerned with the ferry on one particular day. Our truck was heavy. Our weight almost swamped many of them. The ferry in question may or may not have had a security cable – I don't remember. But I do know we were traveling during the rainy season and the rivers were high. We were in tsetse fly country; so Mom wouldn't let me get out of the truck cab. I also recall the ferrymen's loud arguing when we drove onto the ferry. Excited shouts erupted as the ferry got away from them and took off downriver. In panic, some of the ferrymen dove into the river and swam to shore. A few stayed with us, and with Dad helping, they finally steered the ferry to the opposite side of the river and then worked it slowly back upstream by poling and pulling at tree branches and vines along the bank. We eventually arrived at the landing and drove off the ferry. I assume Dad gave the men a larger *matabisi* (tip) than usual.

Our entire trip in the truck across Congo was typical. No paved roads. We encountered few services and even fewer garages or parts houses. Roads were either sand or packed clay. The clay was slippery in the rain. Often the roads were one lane with little room for passing another vehicle. Traffic was negligible; we might only see one or two vehicles per day on some of the roads. Travelers carried their own gasoline, and as much as possible, spare parts. They camped for their overnight stops and used bushes for restrooms.

Breakdowns, dirt roads, inconveniences, ferries, heat or tsetse flies – none of these stopped missionaries from doing what they were called to do: to take the gospel to the ends of the earth – my parents included!

31.

Lessons from a Ditch

Should we slide off the road into a ditch today, we would pull out our cell phones and call a tow truck, which would probably arrive within the hour. We would spend that hour texting friends or playing games on our i-Phone. Finally, we would pay the tow truck driver with our credit card. Not so in the Belgian Congo in 1954.

We were returning to the mission field after furlough and were crossing Congo in the old truck, fully loaded. We had stopped by our old station of Mangungu to pick up stored items and were en route to the Kivu Province in Eastern Congo.

The trip ended up taking about a month because of the mechanical delays along the way. It was rainy season, and the roads were almost impassable – sandy one-lane roads in the prairie and slippery wet clay in the mountainous areas.

On this occasion, we had been unable to find a *gite* (government guesthouse) to camp in; so we kept driving. Our encounter with the ditch was after dark. Rain was falling, and the jungle road was winding and narrow. We slid off the road, deep into the ditch, at a steep angle. We had no way to see if we were on the edge of a cliff or not. Around us lay dark, dense jungle. Dad shut the engine off, and we decided to sit it out till daylight. Because of the slanting angle of the cab, sleep was impossible. Mom was wedged against the passenger door. My 13-year-old body was squeezed between her and Dad, who clamped onto the steering wheel to keep from sliding.

After a bit of this, Mom decided she couldn't breathe so she opened her window. But when we heard something in the dark snuffling and licking its chops, Mom rolled the window back up real quick!

When daylight finally came, we were damp, cold and cramped. We clambered out of the cab to assess our situation. The truck was in mud up to the axles, and we could not possibly drive it out. Dad pulled his motorbike off the back of the truck and left to see if he could get help.

He came back some time later, pushing the bike. A bunch of African men from a village accompanied him. They unloaded our truck, piece by piece. Then they did their synchronized chanting and grunting and literally lifted the truck onto the road. They were happy with the money Dad paid them, and they left singing after re-loading the truck. We were off again.

I learned some important lessons from the ditch. My mother was scared of something after all – I had believed her to be fearless. I learned Dad couldn't do some things by himself – I had believed him to be able to do anything! I learned that three people *could survive* the night in the cab of a truck. While in the cab, we quoted the Bible and sang songs to pass the time. And I learned that God was with us, even in the ditch. He protected us, and He provided help for getting out. Perhaps He had protected us from a more serious accident on the night-time road by delaying us. Yes, I learned a lot in the ditch.

I learned the truth of Psalm 27:1: *"The LORD is my light and my salvation; Whom shall I fear? The LORD is the strength of my life; of whom shall I be afraid?"*

32.

"Please Come to our Village!"

From a form letter to constituents, dated September of 1955

"This is what we heard after leading an evangelistic service in a village near our mission compound of Kamulila, Belgian Congo. We were serving with the Berean Mission and had not been there very many months when this happened. Our grasp of the *Kilega* language was pretty sketchy, and we often worked through an interpreter.

"It was a few weeks before we were able to go back to that village. We went on a Friday and took our truck and seven natives, including a *Kilega* evangelist, a cook and some boys to carry our stuff. This might sound like overkill, but just wait.

"On the way we first had to stop and wait for a bridge to be repaired, and then we proceeded to the end of the road (ten miles). Here we had to leave the truck and go on foot the rest of the way with the boys carrying our cots, food, clothes and teaching supplies.

"This part of Congo is mountainous, and our trail led us past several villages. We climbed steeply uphill and then slid down. We did this for an hour or so. The path was wet, and being clay, it was slippery. We lost count of the number of times we sat down and slid.

"Up over the tops of the tall trees we could see heavy clouds and hear rolling thunder. The natives kept urging us to 'hurry.' Finally, all but Alfani the evangelist went on ahead of us. Then it started to rain, and when it rains in Congo, it pours! We stood under a big tree while Alfani ran to catch up to the boys and get our raincoats. But, of course, we were already soaked by the time he returned with them. If the path was slippery before, you should have seen it now! Finally we got to the village where we received a warm welcome by one and all – each person there wanting to shake our hands.

"We were placed in the village teacher's house where we were able to change into drier clothes and warm up by a fire. We slept well that night.

"The next day we had four meetings in the village. We started at 6 a.m. with an object lesson illustrating the resurrection. At 10 a.m., we went through the village, Ira playing hymns on his saxophone, to gather the children for a flannel graph story time. At 3 p.m. we had another meeting, and one more at 6 p.m. with a picture story for the whole village. At each meeting, Alfani interpreted or explained afterward what he thought we were trying to say in our limited *Kilega*. He has been tutoring us in *Kilega*; so he had a pretty good idea of what we were trying to teach. After the evening service, one woman came in tears and said she wanted to accept this Jesus.

"The people from the village brought us eggs, rice, plantains, peanuts and a chicken. We had our natives fix the rice and chicken their way. It was good, but hot with red peppers. We drank lots of water, even though it was a dark color!

"We started for home after the Sunday morning meeting. As we passed one of the last villages on the way to the truck, a woman ran out and asked us if we were going to pass by without giving them a meeting. As tired as we were, we sat down under a shelter, played the saxophone and gave a short

"Please Come to our Village!"

message. "When we got back to the truck, we found the big chief of the whole area waiting for us with a gift of eggs. Truly the fields are white unto harvest. So many villages, so many lost people, so few missionaries and evangelists. Pray with us to the Lord of the harvest! –Al and Carol Cross"

33.

What's in a Move?

*M*issionaries often get moved. In fact, when I was serving as an adult with S.I.M. (Sudan Interior Mission) in the Ivory Coast, we had our own meaning for S.I.M.: "Sure I'll Move." Often on the mission field, because of personnel going on furlough or work opening in a new area, mission boards might request established missionaries to move to fill the gap.

That is what Berean Mission requested my parents do in 1956. They were asked to move from Kamulila where they had been for several months to Uku, a new mission station George and Ruth Kennedy were opening among a different tribe. My parents had been studying the *Kilega* language and now would have to learn a new one, *Kinguana*.

Mom described *Kinguana* as a shortened version of *Swahili* but was glad to be learning it instead of *Kilega*, which was a word-specific language with tonal inflections. For example, a generic word for "bug" in *Kilega* didn't exist because each type of bug had its own name. Mom wrote that you would be unable to hire a boy to cut the "grass" because, again, *Kilega* had no general word for grass. Each type of grass had its own name. Mom said her brain could get around the *Kinguana* language much easier than around *Kilega*. Languages, especially tonal ones, were hard for her.

The move to Uku was going to be difficult. Our family would be living in a little two-room leaf house (banana leaves tied to a stick frame) for months until Dad could build a new cement block house. Mom and Dad packed our possessions to be stored until the house was finished. They had to pack the items so mildew and bugs would not be able to get into them. In the process of packing, Mom decided to get rid of some worn-out clothes. These were very desirable to the village women, and so she offered them for sale. She couldn't give them away because that would have caused a riot. One old woman, she wrote, was so tickled to get a dress that she ran back to the village and got an egg to pay for it – from under her setting hen. "It was good," Mom wrote, "and we made pancakes for breakfast with it."

One of the available meats in this new area of Uku was monkey meat. I had gotten used to monkey meat because we ate it periodically at boarding school. Mom, however, was prejudiced against it but learned to season it well to make it palatable. One way she prepared it was to grind the meat, add lots of onion and spices and use the mixture in stuffed peppers.

One day Dad said he wanted hamburgers, so Mom ground up some monkey meat and was preparing lunch when a European government official surprised them with a visit. Mom had no choice but to invite him to lunch, knowing full well that only the nationals and missionaries ate monkey! The government official appeared to like the hamburger and requested more before he asked what it was. Dad very quickly said in French, *"C'est viande du pays"* (meat of the land). Then he hastily turned the talk to the beef from Kenya, etc.

Mission conference time came soon, and Mom and Dad left Uku to go for a week to another station where the conference was being held. When they returned home, their leaf house was still standing, but much had been added – mostly bugs and dust. And some things had been removed – rats had eaten half of a pair of Dad's work pants, and the seed corn was gone.

My parents were never tied to material things. God always provided for their needs. I saw this time and again. They never took this provision for granted and were always thankful for it. I am reminded of this verse: *"Do not lay up for yourselves treasures on earth, where moth and rust destroy and where thieves break in and steal; but lay up for yourselves treasures in heaven, where neither moth nor rust destroys and where thieves do not break in and steal."* (Matthew 6:19-21) My parents lived by the verse *"My God shall supply all your need..."* (Philippians 4:19a)

Soldier ants take over!

34.

Soldier Ants in the Walls

It was in the middle of the night, and I was sound asleep in my cot under a mosquito net in the kitchen. I was home from boarding school for summer vacation after finishing seventh grade. My parents were still living in the 200-square-foot banana leaf house at Uku. The house had a lean-to added on that housed a flushing toilet and porcelain tub. The house had no running water, but a barrel of water outside supplied the toilet.

Back to that night: Mom suddenly woke me up, handed me my shoes and a flashlight and yelled, "Run outside!" Dad was already out there, firing up his blowtorch. Armies of carnivorous driver ants, also known as "soldier ants," were invading us. These black ants came from the jungle in organized lines that might stretch for miles. The lines were often several ants across. The ants would raid houses or animal pens, by swarming over and devouring anything living. With their pinchers they would take a bite of flesh. I could hear Dad yipping and Mom swatting, and I proceeded to exit the house as fast as I could.

Dad took the blowtorch and followed the main trail of ants, literally frying them as he went, stopping regularly to pull off an ant that had crawled up his pajama legs. Mom and I found a place where the ground was free of ants. We could *hear* the crunching as the ants ate cockroaches, other insects and maybe even mice inside the leaf walls of our house.

For several hours, Dad blow torched the invading army. Mom and I finally crawled into the cab of our truck to wait. By dawn most of the ants had moved on, and we were able to reclaim our house. I only had a few bites but Dad had many!

These driver ants attack in an organized way. The majority of the army is made up of small ants, but every few inches in their line there is an ant that is twice the normal size. These larger ones are the guards that keep the ants in line until they smell warm flesh. Then the guards probably give a command, and the ants spread out, swarming over and eating the victim. They even are able to overpower a small animal. We heard that in the old days, the Congolese tied their enemies to trees in the jungle and let the driver ants execute them. In fact, the night of this invasion, the ants crossed the moat trap and climbed the poles to our rabbit coop. All that remained of the rabbits were a few bones and hair.

Mother pointed out to me later that morning that "*all things work together for good to those who love God....*" (Romans 8:28). Why, our little leaf house was completely pest-free for once!

35.

The Baboon and the Broomstick

Many baboons, monkeys, chimpanzees and gorillas lived in the Kivu Province. On one of our all-day trips through the jungle to Bukavu to get supplies, I remember a frightening encounter. Our radiator had sprung a leak, and while Dad was repairing it, Mom set up the camp stove behind the car and prepared to cook lunch. After a bit, she looked up from stirring the soup and saw a gorilla standing just a few feet away, quietly watching her. Up front with Dad, I had missed seeing him. Mom cautiously backed up, hustled me into the car and motioned to Dad. Not to be intimidated by an animal, Dad jumped up and down and hollered. Very nonchalantly, the gorilla dropped onto all fours and faded into the trees.

When I was about fourteen, while on summer holiday from school and living with my parents at Uku, I had two pet baboons. The villagers had shot the mothers for food, but knowing the white people might actually pay money for the babies, they brought them to Dad.

They were right. Dad bought them and made a chicken-wire enclosure for them next to our leaf house. The older of the two we called "Jojo" and the newborn baby we named

"Peeps," because He always seemed to just sit and peer at us. He had hit his head on a branch, when falling with his mother after she was shot. That left him somewhat retarded.

    Dad eventually had to put a chicken wire divider in the baboon pen because Jojo incessantly teased poor little Peeps. Peeps was even unable to peel his own banana, and we had to do it for him. Jojo, on the other hand, was too smart for his own good. He liked to hold out a tantalizing bit of banana peel through the chicken wire to attract a chicken. As soon as the chicken got close enough to peck it, he grabbed the chicken around the neck and pinned it against the fence just to hear it squawk!

    Every afternoon we would let the baboons out to run. Peeps would go find Dad and sit on his shoe, hang onto his leg, and ride around wherever Dad went. This was all he wanted to do when out for his recreation time. Not so Jojo. In between chasing chickens, he would come to the front of the house where Mom had carefully nurtured two small beds of marigolds. He would dance and chatter until Mom came to the kitchen door. Then he'd grab a handful of marigold plants and prance off, chattering insolently at her. She would chase him with the broom. This became a daily game for the two of them. At least it was a game for Jojo.

    When we went on furlough, we left the baboons with a boy at the missionary boarding school. The rest of the story is sad. Some villagers stole Peeps, who probably ended up in their stew. Jojo got so smart no one could keep him in any kind of pen – he would figure a way to get out. But when he started doing mischief on his adventures (such as letting the rabbits and chickens out of their cages), I think he probably signed his own death warrant!

    The moral I've come up with for this story is this: *Don't plant marigolds if you have pet baboons.*

36.

Mama's 39th Birthday

My mother was born on Christmas day in 1917. Her parents named her Carol Stella (star); they celebrated Christmas on Christmas Eve and Mom's birthday on Christmas Day. On December 24, 1956, Dad and I decided to make Mom a birthday cake. I was home from school and enjoying my vacation at Uku. We had a wood-burning cook stove in one of the two rooms of our leaf house. I don't know where we sent Mom, but she wasn't there to see our efforts. To start off, we got the fire too hot, and not realizing we could cool it by merely waiting, we tried leaving the oven door ajar while it baked. The cake rose and rose and rose. Then it split open. Then it burned and, of course, stuck to the pan. Frosting covered a lot of the problems, and when we ate the cake on Christmas Day, Mom graciously said it tasted good!

The following is Dad's letter to constituents in the States that Christmas: "As we live here in our little 12x20-foot African grass hut [the leaf house], we can well imagine the little Lord Jesus 'away in a manger.' For our house with a leaf roof and dirt floor is very little more than a stable. However, it is wonderful to think that Christ came to earth and lived in such a place – for us. 'The Son of Man has nowhere to lay His head.' (Luke 9:58) We at least have a bed with an innerspring mattress!

"It is the greatest of privileges that we have of telling the story of Christ's love for sinful man here in Congo. As we look forward to our Christmas service when many natives will walk in from miles away, we realize even more our great responsibility. Just last week, our wash boy accepted the Lord, for which we are rejoicing. He is very quiet and intelligent. After only two weeks of training, he knows how to gas the wringer washing machine, does the laundry and irons with the kerosene iron.

"We have found in the Bakuma people of the Kivu Province a people to take the place of the Bambunda and Bampende that we left behind in the Kasai District. Kangania, the old Christian chief from a village about five miles east of here, has, as the Africans say, 'taken our hearts.'

"Day before yesterday, one of the twenty school boys who walks in daily from there, brought word that Kangania was quite sick, so we drove up to his village. As soon as Chief Kangania had said *Yambo* (Greetings), and without a word about himself, he said we must go across the road to see a Christian woman who was sick.

"After speaking to her and giving her a couple of quinine tablets, we went back to Kangania's, where the first thing he wanted to know was what believers did when a Christian died. We told him Christians celebrate the fact that the believer is in Heaven. Knowing that he was thinking of himself, we assured him we would be glad to come say a few words, share the gospel, and help the family lay the body away. This made him very happy, so leaving him with a few quinine and aspirin and a promise of our prayers for him and the sick woman, we came home."

Chiefs who want a Christian burial, laundry boys who want to become believers, villages that want someone to come and tell them about Jesus – these are the reasons my parents were in Africa. Mom would not have wanted to celebrate her 39th birthday anywhere else in the world!

37.

Openglopish and Other Dialects

Openglopish wopas mopy fopavoporopite lopang opuopage whopen opI wopas gropowoping opup opin thope Copongopo.

When I was in my early teens in Congo, I went away to a boarding school, Berean Mission Academy at Katanti, with about 15 other missionary kids. We were all readers, and some of our favorite books were from the "Sugar Creek Gang" series by Paul Hutchins. These adventure stories were about a gang of Christian boys whose episodes thrilled and inspired us. One of the boys, a tall, gangly, uncoordinated one called "Dragonfly," was always getting the gang in trouble because of his allergies. The boys would be hiding in an effort to solve some mystery, and Dragonfly would sneeze and give them away. He endeared himself to me because of the language he created named *Openglopish*. It was sort of like *Pig-Latin* but spoken by saying the syllable "op" in front of every pronounced vowel.

As we invented games and played in the jungle in our free time, we interwove fact and fiction. Because we were studying the Normans and Saxons in history class, we incorporated them into our play. We divided ourselves into two

so many hats!

groups with complicated rules for capturing each other, securing hideouts, etc. We did this along the intertwining jungle trails going to various African gardens. Because we also were studying French, we chose this as the official language for the Normans. The Saxons – of which I was happily one – used *Openglopish*. We spent all the time we could in the evenings in the dorm practicing and perfecting our *Openglopish*. The final exam was to quote "Peter Piper Picked a Peck of Pickled Peppers" in it. *I can still do it!*

We developed a complicated set of rules. To capture someone from the other side or to free a captive required two from either team. We used birdcalls to communicate with other teammates, letting them know we had been captured or had taken someone captive. I remember one time we Saxons had captured a Norman lad (I think it was Roger Green, a son of our house parents) and tied him to a tree in a Saxon hideout. That was against the rules; we weren't supposed to tie anyone! Then the supper bell rang, and we all ran to the dormitory. Not until we were all seated at the table did we notice Roger's empty chair and remember him!

We spent much of our free time playing in the jungle and making hideouts. Linda Hendry (a teacher's daughter) and I were proud of ourselves when we made a hideout the others couldn't find. We had attached a rope to a branch so it hung down the backside of a big tree beside the trail. Brush grew all around it. We would reach around the tree, grab the rope and swing ourselves around to the back of the tree where we had cleared a path with our machetes to our hideout. I don't remember if we ever told anyone where it was.

I graduated from eighth grade at Katanti in 1956. Two years later, my parents and I returned to America. And this ended the era of hideouts, jungle swings and machetes.

I love reflecting back on those carefree childhood days at Berean Mission Academy when our greatest challenge was to learn *Openglopish*. I can't help but think how serious is the business of missionaries learning a foreign language so that they can communicate God's love to their people group.

Oh, how we need to uphold these missionary apprentices in prayer!

38.

Mama Cross (1917-2012)

From the time she was little, Mom became known as a *helper*. Her family was poor and large, and Mom's lot was to help with the younger siblings. She quickly became an organizer for them, learning the skills she later would use as an adult.

From an early age, I watched Mom continue that role of helper, always assisting Dad with his projects, whether it was doing construction, studying for exams, preparing a sermon, or even repairing a car. She did this self-sacrificially, putting her own projects aside.

On the mission field in the Belgian Congo, the locals on our Mangungu-Luembe station also saw in this white woman the spiritual gift of "helps" They named her in their *Kikongo* language *"Mama Nsadisa,"* meaning "Mama Helper."

Mom was good at teaching. She wrote creatively. She practiced hospitality graciously and generously. She could organize anything within an inch of its life! She was clever in disciplining me. The first (and only) screaming tantrum I threw at age two, she countered by throwing a glass of water in my face. The first time I sassed her, she made me chew a bar of soap!

She also had a great sense of humor. Mom used to tease me with her gift of "skid talking." There were times when I was bored and wanting her company, I would come inside. I often found her reading or working at the table. She might tell me to sit down, and then she'd say something like this: "Why, Margie, just because nothing will come of it, go and open the book that got wet in the rain on that day the picnic was ruined by the dog jumping into the pool under the basement steps while the trees shed their leaves into the pot of chili beans that Archie dumped into the bathtub that came on the ship with Grandpa's piano in a mahogany packing crate banded with metal straps from around the 55-gallon drum that Crisco came in for the hotel restaurant in Ceres where the gas tanker blew up and puncture vines got all the bike tires by the canal great aunt LaVelle swam in wearing her six-piece suit in 1928..." and so on she would continue, hardly taking a breath! I would yell "Mama!" in frustration and go back outside, which is probably what she wanted in the first place.

I remember often seeing my mother at the table grading papers, planning school lessons, writing letters or doing accounts. When I'd ask her what she was doing, she'd always say, "I'm doing business." Oh, how badly I wanted to "do business" like her, and I would set up papers and books on a little table in my room and "do business." I still think of that sometimes when I am at my desk, involved in just that – doing business.

The spiritual gift of "helps" I Corinthians 12:28 describes is the gift Mom radiated. And until she succumbed to Alzheimer's in her later years, she continued to be a helper to me and to anyone who was a part of her life. She will *always* be a role model to me. I miss this special helper terribly.

"Precious in the sight of the Lord is the death of His saints" (Psalm 116:15).

Mama Carol Stella Cross went to be with her Lord on May 10, 2012. I know she is finding something up there to do to be of help because that's who God made her to be. I love you, Mom.

39.

Daddy "Kitoko" Cross (1917-2012)

*I*ra "Al" Cross was given the name *Tata Kitoko (beautiful)* by the people at Mangungu in 1948. To them he was beautiful; he was patient with them, he cared about them and he fixed things for them. In fact, he fixed things for anyone. Missionaries from other stations would send messengers with the word that their generator needed repairing, their car needed fixing, or their musical instruments needed tuning. He could do it all. If he didn't know how to do something, he would read up on it or just go at it. If the necessary part was unavailable, he would make it! Rarely did we visit another mission station that something there didn't need his "fixing."

Dad designated Saturday mornings on the Mangungu station for repairing whatever the village people brought to him. Dad often told about one man who brought in a hand-wound phonograph that didn't work. Dad pulled the top off and discovered there was nothing inside. He explained to the man that without "innards," it couldn't be fixed. The poor man, ignorant of mechanics, couldn't understand that. "Why," he said, "you fixed my friend's bicycle last week." He went away mumbling to himself, sure he had been slighted by Dad!

Dad did all this repair work besides the regular station duties of preaching, teaching, building, supervising workmen, overseeing the dispensary, etc. However, he loved the challenge of fixing things or making them from nothing. We rarely traveled in Congo without serious breakdowns (clutch going out, generator quitting, tires blowing, radiator leaking, or worse). Dad always just took these things in stride and tackled the repair while Mom and I fetched for him or made lunch.

He loved babies and toddlers and often had one in tow or in his arms. They adored him and followed him everywhere.

Dad loved to read. One of the things my parents shipped with them to Congo was a set of Encyclopedia Britannica. Mom and Dad bought them in 1939. They had eloped to get married and had no money for a honeymoon at that time. So they saved up for a weekend in San Francisco at a later date. Arriving in the city, even before checking into a motel, they visited a bookstore and saw the set on sale. They spent their honeymoon money on the encyclopedias and went home! In Congo, Dad used whatever available time he had just *reading* the encyclopedias, often by kerosene lamp in the evenings. He loved to learn about things and could discuss almost any topic because of his vast reading.

Dad was also self-taught on the piano, guitar, violin and saxophone. He used his musical abilities in his missionary work – in the church, in the villages and even on our verandah where he played to impromptu crowds.

Rev. Ira Allen Cross went to be with the Lord on October 11, 2012, in Sonora, California. I learned so much from my Dad, and I miss him a lot. I doubt there is much that needs fixin' in Heaven, but there *is* music, and he would be in the middle of that! I can't wait to hear him play a harp!

Appendix

Languages of the Belgian Congo

French became the official language of Congo when the Belgians colonized the country in 1908. The country has 200 ethnic groups with a current population of 80 million (*Wikipedia*).

As Congolese were forced to work together to build the railway from Matadi (the port city) to the capital city of Leopoldville (now Kinshasa), a trade language grew. It was an abbreviated language called *Kituba, Kikongo* or *Kikwango*, depending on the region. *Kituba* ("small part") had a vocabulary of 300 words. *Kikongo* currently lists about 10,000 words. The hand-typed, stapled *Kikwango* dictionary that Mom and Dad used at Mangungu listed 1,800 words.

Compare that with our own English. Internet research in 2016 tells us that about one million word forms are in our English dictionary of which more than 171,000 are presently used words; the average person has a vocabulary of more than 20,000 words.

In 2005, at African negotiations in Sun City, South Africa, when the new Congo constitution was formed, the leadership adopted five national languages: *French, Lingala, Swahili, Tshiluba* and *Kikongo*.

"*Kituba* was sufficient for trading purposes, but it was inadequate as a vehicle for conveying the Holy Scriptures. Several missions (notably the American Mennonite Brethren) working in the Kwango District of Congo, collaborated to develop and improve the word forms and vocabulary in order to produce the New Testament" *(Ira Cross)*. The *Kikwango* version called *Luwawanu Yampa* was printed by the British and American Bible Societies in 1950. It was distributed in our area in 1951.

About the Author

My Story

I feel blessed by my heritage of having had parents who loved the Lord and served Him. My life being an MK was not always easy or fun, but I was proud of my parents and glad to be part of their experiences in the Belgian Congo.

My mother home-schooled me for the second grade, after which I went away to boarding school. I returned to the United States for my junior year of high school, graduating in 1959 from Ceres Union High in California.

In 1965, after I completed the diploma course from Multnomah School of the Bible in Portland, Oregon, I stayed and worked on staff in the printing department, continuing my art education in night classes at Portland State University and Portland Community College. In 1967, during a missionary conference message by Luis Palau, God called me to return to Africa as a missionary artist.

At that time, my parents were with Sudan Interior Mission, working in Dahomey (Benin). They told me about S.I.M.'s need for an artist for a new evangelistic publication called (in French) *"Champion."* A number of other godly friends told me about *Champion* as well, seeing me as the perfect candidate. I applied to S.I.M., was accepted, and in 1968 was on my way to France for French language study at the *Centre de Formation Missionaire* in Albertville for a few months.

In Africa, I worked for one year in Lagos, Nigeria, doing illustrations and page layouts for the *Champion Magazine*. It was published in French for distribution to the twenty-two French-speaking countries of Africa. The entire staff of the Champion Magazine was transferred to the Evangelical Publications Center in Abidjan, Ivory Coast, at the end of that year. I spent another nine years as art editor for that organization.

I returned to America in 1978 and worked in the graphic arts field, mostly free-lancing. I met John Wall at my home church, Hinson Memorial Baptist, in Portland, Oregon. He had come to Portland from Montana to attend Western Conservative Baptist Seminary. In 1986, we were married. We are both retired now and living in Waldport, a charming little hamlet on the central Oregon Coast. Completing this book of my experiences in the Congo is the fulfillment of a long-time dream. I pray that all who read it will be blessed.

Margie Wall, 2016
Waldport, Oregon

In Grateful Recognition

For my husband, **John Wall**, who has supported and encouraged me by taking over housework and fielding the phone calls on my "book" days. And he has been my computer technical support!

For my "brothers" and "sisters" in the **Eickmeyer** family. **Alice Eickmeyer** gave me the prod I needed to keep going on the book; with her library science degree she has given invaluable and qualified counsel. **Joyce Eickmeyer Motis** and her husband, **Harvey,** made their cozy Springfield home available on their vacation trips so we could get away to work undisturbed. **Carol Eickmeyer** let us use her St. Helens home for the final preparation of the manuscript. And **Rev. Glen Eickmeyer** wrote the foreword for this book.

For my sister, **Jeannie Cross Bowen**, who has encouraged me all through the project; she added her expertise and memories to it.

For my many proofreaders: **Barbara Wild**, pastor's wife and mentor, the first official proofreader of the manuscript. **Debbie Eickmeyer**, Glen's wife, who did additional proofreading. **Barbara Darland,** who gave some excellent copyediting advice, and **Ann Staatz,** who did the final copyediting of the book.

For **Clement "Bud" Kroeker** who, with his background and knowledge of Congo, provided valuable information for the maps. And for **Bill Lawson** who assisted with his computer expertise.

For **Pastor Mike Hale** and the congregation of First Baptist Church, Waldport, Oregon, for their kudos when I shared some of the stories in "Missionary Moments" during the worship services. Their enthusiasm has been a huge encouragement.

For **Sally Morris** and the other "**Women of Joy**" at Waldport who have allowed me to read the stories of *"So Many Hats"* as devotionals at our monthly craft workshops. They have spurred me on to complete the project.

And finally, for all those who assisted me financially in the publishing of this book. May God bless you all!

Related Books on Congo Missions

Anderson, Viola P, "A Gleam of Light in Congo's Night" (Congo Gospel Mission publishers, Villa Park, Illinois, 1949) 88 pages. *The story of the beginning of the Congo Gospel Mission in Congo.*

Dunkelberger, Stella C, "Crossing Africa – in a Missionary Way" (Westbrook Publishing Company, Philadelphia, PA, 1935) 105 pp. *The home secretary of UTM visits African missions, including Mangungu.*

Kroeker, Joanne, "Shiny Shoes on Dusty Paths" (Treasure House of Destiny Publishers, Shippensburg, PA, 1995) ISBN 1-56043-845-2, 274 pp. Biography of Abe and Mary Kroeker.

Kroeker, Joanne, "Shiny Shoes on Dusty Paths, Vol. II" (CT Publishing Co, Philadelphia, PA, 1996) ISBN 1-56226-317-X, 285 pp. Continued biography of Abe and Mary Kroeker.

Loewen, Melvin J, "Three Score, the Story of an Emerging Mennonite Church in Central Africa" (Congo Inland Mission, Elkhart, Indiana, 1972)

Unrau, Kornelia, "My Years in Congo" (self-published, 20 pages). The story of a Mennonite nurse in Congo who was evacuated in the 1960 independence. *Kornelia Unrau is the sister of H.H. Unrau, the maternal grandfather of Margie Wall's husband, John.*

Lightning Source UK Ltd.
Milton Keynes UK
UKHW022043060722
405471UK00005B/429